A PADDLER'S GUIDE TO
ALGONQUIN PARK

A PADDLER'S GUIDE TO
ALGONQUIN PARK

KEVIN CALLAN

The BOSTON
MILLS PRESS

A BOSTON MILLS PRESS BOOK

First printing, 2012

National Library of Canada Cataloguing in Publication

Callan, Kevin
A paddler's guide to Algonquin Park / Kevin Callan. -- 2nd ed.

Previously published under title: Brook trout and blackflies :
a paddler's guide to Algonquin Park.
Includes bibliographical references.

ISBN-13: 978-1-77085-058-3

1. Canoes and canoeing--Ontario--Algonquin Provincial
Park--Guidebooks. 2. Algonquin Provincial Park (Ont.)--
Guidebooks. I. Title.

GV776.15.A7C34 2012   797.12209713'147   C2011-906736-6

Publisher Cataloging-in-Publication Data (U.S.)

Callan, Kevin.
A paddler's guide to Algonquin Park : Kevin Callan.
2nd ed.

[176] p. : col. photos., col. maps ; cm.
Includes bibliographical resources.
Summary: Color maps and photographs are used to describe
a variety of Algonquin's paddling routes, from true wilderness
adventures to less rustic excursions.

ISBN-13: 978-1-77085-058-3 (pbk.)

1. Canoes and canoeing -- Ontario – Algonquin. 2. Provincial Park --
Guidebooks. 3. Algonquin Provincial Park (Ont.) -- Guidebooks.
I. Title.

797.122/09713 dc23   GV776.15.O57C355   2012

Published by
BOSTON MILLS PRESS

IN CANADA:
Distributed by Firefly Books Ltd.
66 Leek Crescent
Richmond Hill, Ontario, Canada L4B 1H1

IN THE UNITED STATES:
Distributed by Firefly Books (U.S.) Inc.
P. O. Box 1338, Ellicott Station
Buffalo, New York, USA 14205

Cover design by Hartley Millson
Interior design by Mary Firth
Photographs by the author
Maps by Mary Firth and Kevin Callan

The publisher gratefully acknowledges
the financial support for our publishing
program by the Government of Canada
through the Canada Book Fund as
administered by the Department of
Canadian Heritage.

Printed in China

Contents

Nipissing River, one of the more remote canoe routes in Algonquin.

Preface

I HAD JUST DOUSED THE EVENING FIRE AND was walking toward the tent to curl up inside my cozy sleeping bag for the night when I heard it — a single wolf howl. The haunting cry of the wolf lured me into my canoe and I paddled quietly down the weedy shoreline toward the echoing call.

A few minutes later I stopped paddling and gave out a long, drawn-out howl. Immediately I heard a response coming from the nearby roadway. In hopes of spotting the canine, I dipped my paddle blade into the water and pushed my canoe slowly around a rock outcrop. To my surprise, instead of a wolf, I came upon a group of over two hundred campers standing along the shoreline in silence as a park interpreter sounded out a third howl.

Not wanting to be discovered, I slipped back behind the point and waited there in silence until the crowd moved back toward the road. I sheepishly paddled back to my campsite feeling somewhat cheated out of my wilderness experience.

Let's face it, at times, canoeing Algonquin can be downright frustrating. I've had bombers from the Petawawa Air Base scare me silly as they flew low over my campsite on Pen Lake; I've had to clamber through an entanglement of logging roads and railway tracks along a portage; I've photographed moose equipped with radio collars; and I've dealt with nuisance bears with colored tags clipped to their ears. I've also spent countless hours pushing the redial button on my telephone trying to make a reservation on my favorite lake, only to get through and find out that it was completely booked. Even after I was finally able to reserve a spot, I was forced to line up at the gatehouse to receive a list of rules and regulations before I could push my way through the crowds on the portage.

So why do I bother? Why do I still spend every possible moment paddling and portaging Algonquin's semi-wilderness? Because, for me, this 2,955 square miles (7,653 sq km) of Central Ontario parkland holds innumerable memories: photographing a merganser mom as it tried to lead seventeen fluffy ducklings along the shoreline in a straight line; watching as a trophy-size trout gurgled up to the surface of the river to snatch the fly on the end of my line; waking up on time to see the early-morning mist blanket the lake around my island campsite; and sleeping under the rustic remains of a ranger cabin as a storm was building outside. One of my most unforgettable memories is the moment I caught a quick glimpse of a real wolf lapping up the tea-colored water of the less-traveled Nipissing River.

This book is both a collection of my memories and a guide to places where you can escape to gather your own.

Anywhere a large number of canoeists gather there is a lengthy list of rules to follow. There is, of course, a ban on bottles, cans, chain saws, radios, firearms and motorboats on the majority of lakes, and a valid interior camping permit must be carried at all times. The permit allows up to nine canoeists (local camps traditionally traveled three per canoe) to camp at any designated site marked by an orange sign. At each access point you must lay out your projected route to the gate-house attendant, and you must keep to it, especially within Controlled Camping Zones (lakes within a day's travel from the put-in).

Equally important to park rules is canoe-camping etiquette. On a portage (marked by yellow signs), the person carrying the canoe should always be given the right of way (even if the canoe is made of lightweight Kevlar). Also, be sure never to block either the put-in or the take-out with gear or canoes while carrying across a portage. In camp, dishwashing and hair washing should be done at the back of the site, away from the lake, and a stack of dry wood should be left behind for the next campers. Finally, keep the noise to a minimum: no wolf howling after midnight!

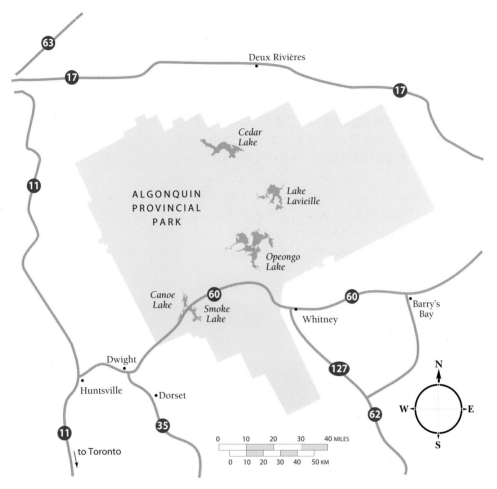

Acknowledgments

Writing this book would have been impossible without the help of many people. I would first like to thank my canoe companions who tagged along for the fieldwork for this book: Scott Roberts, Mike Walker, Doug Galloway, Peter Fraser, John Glasgow, Dave Hicks, John Buck, Kerry Buck, Deborah Chatsis, Fred, Maggie and Hilary Bakker, the canoeheads at Boston Mills (Noel Hudson, John Denison and James Bosma), and especially my wife, Alana, who carried the heaviest of our two packs along the 5,800-yard (5,305 m) Dickson/Bonfield portage.

Special thanks also to Mary Firth, mapmaker and designer extra-ordinaire; editor Kathy Fraser; to Hikers Haven for being behind me since day one; Mike Cullen and the staff at Trent Photographics for their expertise; the gang at Wild Rock Outfitters for all of their enthusiasm; the friendly ministry staff posted at each permit office; and Algonquin Outfitters, who let me test-drive the odd Swift Canoe during the past few years.

Finally, I would like to thank my parents for all of their support through the years, and for allowing a nature nut like me to grow up to be a full-fledged Algonquinite.

Enjoying a quick lunch break (Sunbeam Lake).

Canoe Lake Circuit

SINCE THE ESTABLISHMENT OF THE PARK IN 1893, Canoe Lake has been a prominent access point for canoe trippers. The wilderness setting and the lake's close proximity to Algonquin's major waterways attracted lodges, youth camps and leaseholder's cabins to the area, and along with them, many keen canoeists.

Today the Canoe Lake Circuit is the most popular canoe route in Algonquin Park. In fact, the lake has become so cluttered with canoeists that it has been nicknamed "Yonge Street." But modern-day paddlers are no longer attracted to Canoe Lake for its wilderness appeal alone. Instead, many now come to explore the ruins of their predecessors and capture a sense of Algonquin's rich past in this giant outdoor museum.

The road leading off Highway 60 to the Canoe Lake access point is marked to the left, 8.7 miles (14 km) east of the West Gate, and canoeists can either put in at the beach or at the docks beside the Portage Store.

Once heading north on Canoe Lake, the first museum exhibit to visit is the remains of Camp Wapomeo, the sister of camp Ahmek (the first Canadian-owned private camp in Algonquin).

Taylor Statten, who first visited Canoe Lake during a family canoe trip in 1913 and later took a lease for a summer home on Little Wapomeo Island, developed both youth camps. Camp Ahmek, for boys, opened in 1921 and was located on the beach at the end of the northeast bay (surveyor Alexander Murray stopped on this beach to build birchbark canoes during his expedition of 1853 and gave the lake its name). Camp Wapomeo, for girls, was initiated three years later, with Taylor's wife, Ethel, acting as director.

South Tea Lake was the original proposed site of the girls' camp, but Ethel refused to have her camp so far away from Ahmek; so Taylor decided to expand onto the family's cottage on Little Wapomeo Island. Fearing a scandal would ensue over boys and girls sharing the same lake, the entire board of directors resigned shortly after.

It's no secret that a few mischievous acts did occur. Boys from Camp Pathfinder, on Source Lake, once painted their canoes green and gray — Camp Wapomeo's colors — and, suitably camouflaged, closed in on the camp to catch a glimpse of the skinny-dipping girls. But high jinks aside, both camps prospered, and Camp Wapomeo eventually expanded to the larger island to the south.

The Canoe Lake museum tour continues to the northwest of Big

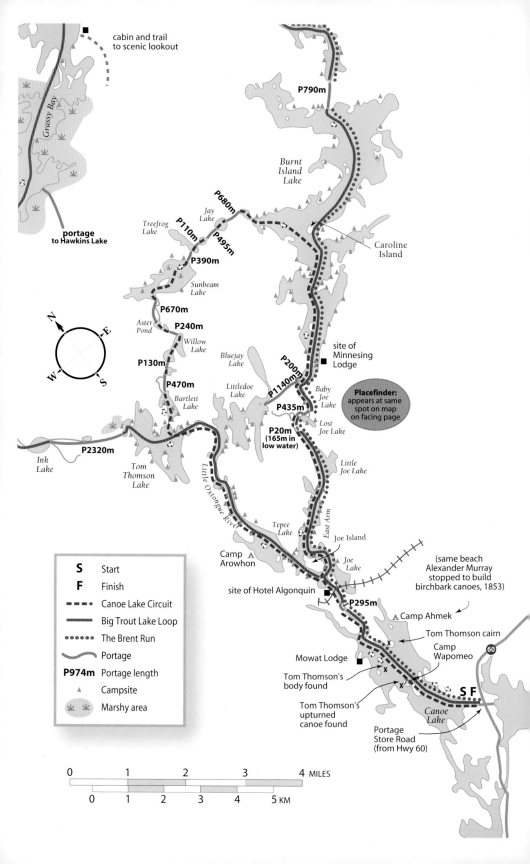

cabin and trail
to scenic lookout

Grassy Bay

**portage
to Hawkins Lake**

P790m

*Burnt
Island
Lake*

*Jay
Lake* **P680m**

*Treefrog
Lake* **P110m**

P495m

P390m

Caroline
Island

*Sunbeam
Lake*

P670m

*Aster
Pond* **P240m**

*Willow
Lake*

P130m

*Bluejay
Lake*

P200m

site of
Minnesing
Lodge

P1140m

Placefinder:
appears at same
spot on map
on facing page

P470m

*Littledoe
Lake*

*Bartlett
Lake*

P435m

*Baby
Joe Lake*

**P20m
(165m in
low water)**

*Lost
Joe Lake*

*Little
Joe Lake*

P2320m

*Ink
Lake*

*Tom
Thomson
Lake*

Little Oxtongue River

*Tepee
Lake*

East Arm

Joe Island

Camp
Arowhon

*Joe
Lake*

(same beach
Alexander Murray
stopped to build
birchbark canoes, 1853)

site of Hotel Algonquin

P295m

▲ Camp Ahmek

60

Tom Thomson cairn

Camp
Wapomeo

Mowat Lodge

Tom Thomson's
body found

Tom Thomson's
upturned
canoe found

Portage
Store Road
(from Hwy 60)

*Canoe
Lake*

S F

N
W E
S

S	Start
F	Finish
- - -	Canoe Lake Circuit
———	Big Trout Lake Loop
••••	The Brent Run
∿∿∿	Portage
P974m	Portage length
▲	Campsite
🌿	Marshy area

0   1   2   3   4 MILES

0   1   2   3   4   5 KM

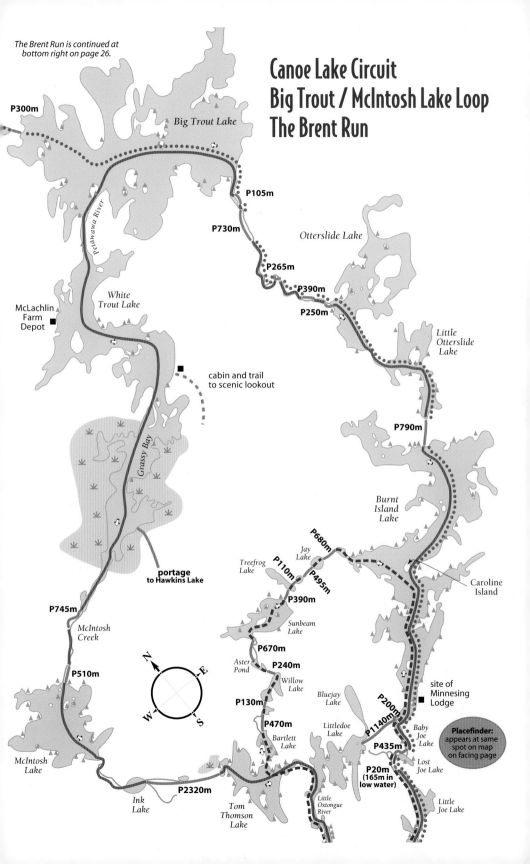

The Brent Run is continued at bottom right on page 26.

P300m

Canoe Lake Circuit
Big Trout / McIntosh Lake Loop
The Brent Run

Big Trout Lake

P105m

P730m

Otterslide Lake

P265m

P390m

P250m

White Trout Lake

Petawawa River

McLachlin Farm Depot

Little Otterslide Lake

cabin and trail to scenic lookout

P790m

Grassy Bay

Burnt Island Lake

P680m

Jay Lake

Treefrog Lake

P110m

P495m

Caroline Island

portage to Hawkins Lake

P390m

P745m

McIntosh Creek

Sunbeam Lake

P670m

Aster Pond

P240m

N

E

W

S

P510m

Willow Lake

Bluejay Lake

site of Minnesing Lodge

P130m

P200m

Placefinder: appears at same spot on map on facing page

P1140m

Littledoe Lake

Baby Joe Lake

P470m

Bartlett Lake

P435m

McIntosh Lake

P20m (165m in low water)

Lost Joe Lake

P2320m

Ink Lake

Tom Thomson Lake

Little Oxtongue River

Little Joe Lake

Canoe Lake's memorial to Tom Thomson.

Wapomeo Island at the townsite of Mowat. The village of the Gilmour Lumber Mills (which ran between 1892 and 1897) once housed over seven hundred people. But the boomtown slowly went bust; now all that remains are crumbled foundations and a small graveyard perched up on a hill.

Mr. Shannon Frazer, the past postmaster of Mowat, with the help of his wife, refurbished the old bunkhouse into Mowat Lodge. In May 1912, a year before the resort was actually opened for business, artist Tom Thomson and his friend, H. B. Jackson, became unofficial guests when their first canoe trip into the park was delayed due to high winds.

Mowat Lodge later became Thomson's base as he spent time searching out sketch sites. It was here, on July 8, 1917, that the artist was last seen before his drowned body was recovered eight days later, floating off Kiowa Rocks at Big Wapomeo Island.

The apparent drowning has always been the subject of great speculation. The autopsy performed by Dr. G. W. Howland, who dis-covered Thomson's body, found no trace of water in the lungs. There was also a bruise on the left temple and fishing line wrapped around the leg. Some believe that Martin Bletcher, who had feelings for Thomson's secret lover, Winnie Trainer, mur-dered him after a quarrel. Others infer that Shannon Frazer, of Mowat Lodge, owed Thomson money, and, after an argument, knocked him over the head, hauled Thomson's body into the canoe, and floated him out into the lake.

A commemorative cairn was built by the artist's friends on a hill above his favorite Canoe Lake campsite. The site is almost directly across from Mowat, on the west side of the lake's northern point. Look for a colorful totem pole peering through the trees, which was erected alongside the cairn in 1930 by the Taylor Statten camps. It depicts and commemorates Thomson's achievements and death.

The route heads north from the cairn to where Canoe Lake splits into two channels. Keep to the right and head toward the first portage of the trip. The well-worn path, leading to Joe Lake, is marked to the left of a cement dam. Take note, however, that this 325-yard (295 m) portage has long been one of the busiest in the park (in 1967, during a holiday weekend, ninety-six canoes were counted here). To avoid this kind of traffic jam at the take-out, and to shorten your carry, use the side trail farther upstream, provided water levels are high enough. Between the dam and a railway bridge that can be seen from the put-in, at the crest of a hill along the left shore, is the former site of Hotel Algonquin. The hotel, built in 1905 by Tom Merrill, of Rochester, New York, was one of the many lodges located along the rail-way that ran through the park. With the phasing out of the railway during the 1950s, however, the hotel became obsolete, and in 1957 the park staff burnt it to the ground.

Joe Lake is just beyond the bridge, with the route making its way to the right of Joe Island and then heading east along the elongated inlet into Little Joe Lake. A narrow creek with a 22-yard (20 m) lift-over (or 180-yard [165 m] portage in low water conditions), marked immediately to the right for when water levels are low, must then be navigated to where a 475-yard (435 m) portage, marked on the left bank, takes you into Baby Joe Lake. Like the first portage, it can be shortened by continuing upstream and poling or wading your way to Lost Joe Lake. A short trail to the left of the rock-strewn rapids that run into the lake is then used.

There's just one more portage before Burnt Island Lake. It is located on the opposite end of Baby Joe Lake. Two portages are marked at the take-out: a 1,250-yard (1,140 m) trail that heads into Littledoe Lake, and a short, 220-yard (200 m) trail to the right heads into Burnt Island Lake.

Once on Burnt Island Lake, be sure to walk up the short trail directly across from the campsite at the outlet and explore the former site of the Minnesing Lodge. This lodge was one of two cedar-log resorts built by the Grand Trunk Railway in 1913 to serve as outpost camps away from the more civilized Highland Inn on Cache Lake. A Canadian National Railways brochure described it as "an ideal vacation place in the heart of an immense wilderness." It was accessible by either a rough, bumpy stagecoach ride from Cache Lake or by canoe and guide by way of Joe Lake.

In 1923, Minnesing Lodge was turned into a bible school. It was dismantled in 1954 when the Ministry of Natural Resources (MNR) developed a policy to phase out some of the lodges in Algonquin. The "immense wilderness" still remains, however, and Burnt Island Lake is an excellent place to spend your first night.

The last time I paddled the Canoe Lake circuit I went alone and chose a prime campsite on Burnt Island Lake, near Caroline Island. Exhausted from an all-day struggle against a constant gale, I pulled the canoe up on shore and lit the campstove to make tea. I erected my tent, walked into the backwoods to hang my bear rope over an outstretched limb of a gnarled pine, and then rummaged through my food pack for the evening meal — a spicy Moroccan couscous, with carrot cake for dessert. It was my first solo trip of the season, and, as always, the moment the sun began to set I started to become uneasy with my surroundings. Not exactly easing my nerves was a persistent raccoon who made numerous sneak attacks on my food bag. We took turns chasing each other out of the campsite until I finally gave up on dessert and strung up my supplies in the tree, wondering what I had done to deserve this treatment.

I got a good laugh the next morning when I noticed that the canoeists camped across from me were being harassed by the same raccoon. My sense of poetic justice was restored when I saw that they were both wearing coonskin hats.

From Burnt Island Lake, the route circles back through a series of small lakes and ponds. The first of eight connecting portages is found at the west end of Burnt Island's large central bay, north of Caroline Island. The 745-yard (680 m) trail is the longest and hardest en route, with an abrupt hill not far from the take-out.

It was on this portage, while straining to clamber up the steep slope, that I caught scent of a carcass rotting somewhere nearby. Sickened by the stench, but curious, I wedged the canoe in the crook of a tree and walked off the trail, heading in the direction of the awful smell.

It was a good twenty minutes before I found it — a woefully thin cow moose with its intestines, ridden with flies, spread out across the forest floor. Its hair had also been scraped away, a sure sign of moose tick infestation and most likely the cause of death. In early spring, many moose die from hypothermia after the ticks have overrun their hosts.

From Jay Lake, three more portages remain before scenic Sunbeam Lake — an excellent place to stop for lunch. The first two — a 540-yard (495 m) portage into an unnamed oval pond, and a 120-yard (110 m) portage leading into Treefrog Lake — are relatively flat. The 425-yard (390 m) portage out of Treefrog, however, is cursed with both a steep take-out and put-in.

After snacking on soup and sandwiches at one of the small islands out in the middle of Sunbeam Lake, continue west to the first of another series of portages. The take-out is marked to the right of a marshy outlet. This 735-yard (670 m) portage, leading to Aster Pond, is confusing at times; the path crosses over the stream twice, with a number of side trails that lead around mucky sections right up to the put-in at a gigantic beaver dam.

Aster Pond is a quick paddle, with another steep portage (260 yards [240 m]) waiting at the end that takes you into Willow Lake. The last two portages of the day — a 140-yard (130 m) portage into a stagnant pond cluttered with rotten stumps, and a 515-yard (470 m) portage into Bartlett Lake — are fairly easy.

To reach Tom Thomson Lake from Bartlett Lake, simply paddle across to the opposite end and through the narrow channel. First called Black Bear Lake, this lake was renamed on the initiative of the Canadian Federation of

Canoe Lake Circuit

TIME
2 to 3 days

DIFFICULTY
Novice

PORTAGES
13

LONGEST PORTAGE
745 yards
(680 m)

Artists in 1946. Whether Thomson favored the lake is not known; however, he did visit the area numerous times during his travels in the park.

I arrived on Tom Thomson Lake in early afternoon, aided by a tailwind throughout the day, and set up camp on a rock point in the northern bay. I took advantage of this raccoon-free site and baked yesterday's dessert as an appetizer before dinner. I later spotted a deer browsing on some marsh grass directly across from my campsite, adding to an already perfect day. I silently reached for my camera and attached the zoom lens. Then, to my utter amazement, two curious otters walked into the frame. Of course, when I got the film back from the developer a week later, both the otters and the deer were out of focus.

The trip back to the Canoe Lake is only a half-day's paddle, giving you ample time for the drive home. From Tom Thomson Lake, head southeast down the channel leading to Littledoe Lake. Then, make a right and continue along a narrow passage to Tepee Lake.

Your last look into Algonquin's past is Camp Arowhon, at the west shore of Tepee Lake. Ernest Thompson Seton and Ellsworth Jaeger opened the Camp of the Red Gods here in 1931, but it lasted only a year. Lillian Kates then opened Camp Arowhon, in 1934, and later built the Arowhon Pines Lodge, on Little Joe Lake, to house visiting parents. Camp Arowhon and the Taylor Statten camps on Canoe Lake are the only Algonquin camps that have been owned and operated by the same family for three generations.

Joe Lake is to the south of Tepee Lake and is the last of the chain of portage-free lakes. Once on Joe Lake, keep to the right shoreline to get back to the railway bridge and 320-yard (295 m) portage around the cement dam. While paddling back across Canoe Lake, keep a watchful eye out for the ghost of Tom Thomson, last seen haunting the shore of Big Wapomeo Island in his pale blue canoe.

Big Trout Lake Loop

BIG TROUT LAKE HAS IT ALL: BREATHTAKING LAKES, swamps teeming with wildlife, excellent campsites, fantastic fishing, easy portages and quick access. The only problem is that everyone seems to know about it.

There are ways to avoid the masses, however. By going out during early spring or late fall you can avoid the crowds brought in by the neighboring camps during prime season. My wife, Alana, and I, only able to find time to paddle the loop during mid-August, found that by coming to Canoe Lake during midweek we were able to avoid rush-hour traffic not only on the highway, but while loading up at the put-in site as well.

To reach the access point, turn north off Highway 60 onto the road leading to the Portage Store. The gatehouse is down on the beach, near the parking area.

For your first day out, the route heads up from Canoe Lake to Burnt Island Lake (see Canoe Lake Circuit for a route description). From here, you can either spend your first night on Burnt Island Lake or make the extra pilgrimage to Little Otterslide and Otterslide Lakes by way of the 865-yard (790 m) portage. The trail is flat, but watch your footing on the exposed rocks near the put-in.

With no winds to slow our progress, Alana and I made it to Little Otterslide on our first night out. To escape the main stream of traffic out on the lake, we chose an out-of-the-way campsite on the east side of the large island. It was a great spot, except for a nuisance red squirrel who ran off with our entire supply of GORP (Good Old Raisins and Peanuts) and one highly valued chocolate bar.

Early the next morning, we paddled on from Little Otterslide Lake into Otterslide Lake by way of a weedy channel and then headed to the northwest corner and the beginning of Otterslide Creek. The first portage (275 yards [250 m]) is marked right at the entranceway to the creek, to the left of a giant logjam. It is soon followed by a 425-yard (390 m) portage to the right and a 290-yard (265 m) portage to the left.

Below the last series of portages is a one-mile (1.5 km) section dominated by sedge and tamarack. Here, Alana and I were lucky enough to spot a pair of otters — standing high in the water, their heads up like periscopes — spying on us from a swampy bay. A bull moose also blocked our way for a good ten minutes, and we spooked three great blue herons that were feeding in the shallows.

McIntosh Lake was a favorite stopover for many of Algonquin's first rangers.

Just before the next portage, the shoreline sedge is taken over by a patch of alder. The 800-yard (730 m) trail is marked to the left of where the creek flushes alongside a towering cliff, which can be seen across the waterway halfway along the portage.

The last portage along Otterslide Creek is only 115 yards (105 m) and works its way downhill to the right of a small cascade. A ten-minute paddle down a shallow inlet brings you out into Big Trout Lake.

The route now heads northwest to the third large bay, where a narrow channel joins Big Trout Lake with White Trout Lake. At this point in the trip, with the size of the lakes helping to spread out the crowds of canoeists, Alana and I were able to feel somewhat secluded. For two full days we explored the expanse of both lakes, and the wisps of smoke from distant campfires come dusk were the only sign of other human activity.

From White Trout's southwest end, the route continues through Grassy Bay (watch for the government signs and reflector tape mark-ing the way through this massive wetland) and then up McIntosh Creek, complete with an 815-yard (745 m) portage marked to the right and a 560-yard (510 m) portage marked to the left.

A storm was drifting in from the west when Alana and I reached the end of the last portage, and with the first flash of lightning we made a beeline to the nearest island campsite on McIntosh Lake. Once on shore, we strung up a tarp and sat back to back on top of our packs, holding up the sagging nylon with our paddles. We watched in amazement as forks of lightning lit up the blackened sky (we later learned that during the same thunderstorm, lightning struck a group of Queen's University students camped on Shirley Lake, killing one and injuring three others).

Ten minutes later, the towering clouds drifted east, dragging the sheet of rain with them. Alana and I were able to find enough relatively dry wood on the island to make an adequate fire for drying out our sneakers and socks. Having escaped the downpour, we set about trying to make our campsite as comfortable as our living room back home. We were just settled in when the canoeists from hell came knocking at our door.

A dozen strong, the group of teenagers and its leaders had invaded the far side of the island and immediately began setting up camp. I calmly walked over to the bedraggled bunch, who had obviously not weathered the storm as well as Alana and I, and politely informed the two adults of the group that the island site was already occupied. At first, both leaders ignored me and continued to instruct the misguided youths to erect their tents and tarps directly beside our latrine. Then, after I explained again that they were setting

Algonquin is a paradise for the trout angler.

up camp on a non-designated site, the two adults answered me with a barrage of profanity. I held my tongue, knowing that a feud would only make matters worse, and Alana and I tried to turn a blind eye to our unwelcome guests as they proceeded to make our island look as though the circus had come to town.

Needless to say, we left the island site early the next morning, paddling through thick fog toward the south end of McIntosh Lake and the mouth of Ink Creek. As we entered the brown-stained waterway, we caught the sound of an elongated howl breaking through the mist. At first, we assumed it to be a repeat performance of our nuisance neighbors' nightly party sounds. But after a second howl echoed across the lake, we began to consider the possibility that this baritone voice was that of a genuine Algonquin wolf.

Seconds later, two more wolves joined in, creating a chilling harmony of descending tones. We sat dumbfounded for at least twenty minutes before paddling on. Before long, we came across an open bog lined with miniature tamarack, clumps of insect-eating pitcher plants, and leatherleaf — all decorated with an irregular meshwork of spider webs. The morning made us quickly forget the problems we encountered back at the campsite.

The creek ends at Ink Lake, and on the opposite shore is the longest and roughest portage en route. The 2,540-yard (2,320 m) trail begins with an abrupt hill and then continues through muddy ravines, up a number of steep slopes, and finally, across a soggy field. Fortunately, each major obstruction is equipped with either a wooden staircase or a well-positioned catwalk to ease your way across.

The portage ends in a small bay hidden on the north end of Tom Thomson Lake. Once there, Alana and I ended the trip by heading south to Littledoe Lake and then southwest across Fawn, Tepee, Joe and Canoe Lakes.

Big Trout Lake Loop

TIME
4 to 5 days

DIFFICULTY
Moderate to novice tripping experience

PORTAGES
14

LONGEST PORTAGE
2,540 yards (2,320 m)

*One of the main advantages of canoe tripping in Algonquin
is having the luxury of a well-maintained portage.*

The Brent Run

THE BRENT RUN CANOE RACE WAS INITIATED AFTER rumors that, during the early 1930s, the Stringer boys paddled their cedar-strip canoe from Canoe Lake to Brent and back again in twenty-four hours. Bill Stoqua and Bill Little, both former guides in the park, decided to try their luck and completed their trip in thirty-two hours. Then, on a dare from the two Bills, Hank Laurier and his brother, who were working for the Taylor Statten camps at the time, came in at twenty-seven hours, fueled by only two peanut-butter-and-jelly sandwiches and two cans of orange juice.

The best recorded time to date is twenty-three hours, held by past members of Camp Ahmek Chuck Beamish and Bob Anglin. I'm not suggesting that you go out in a weighted cedar-strip and try to outdo Chuck and Bob. In fact, I recommend that you take a bit more time to complete the trip — eight days.

Canoe Lake is the starting line. To reach the access, turn north off Highway 60 toward the Portage Store. The gatehouse is down on the beach, near the parking area. From Canoe Lake, head north into Burnt Island Lake (see Canoe Lake Circuit for details) and either spend your first night here or portage 865 yards (790 m) into Little Otterslide and Otterslide Lakes. (As Burnt Island is overused, I prefer going the extra stretch.)

From the northwest corner of Otterslide, the route continues north into Big Trout by way of Otterslide Creek using five flat but sometimes muddy portages (275, 425, 290, 800 and 115 yards [250, 390, 265, 730 and 105 m]). Between the third and fourth portage, on the eastern side of the creek, is a scenic cliff; peregrine falcons were last seen nesting here in 1962.

The last of the portages on Otterslide Creek takes you to the right of a picture-perfect cascade. A short paddle from the put-in, up a narrow inlet, is the breathtaking Big Trout Lake.

Big Trout is a large lake, and if winds come up it may be difficult to paddle across to the northern end, so make sure you head out early. Cross the expanse of water to the 330-yard (300 m) portage into Longer Lake, located just west of two small islands. Don't mistake the unmarked path on the opposite side of the islands as the portage; it leads into a small pond fed by twin creeks, and even though it will eventually take you into Longer Lake, the marked portage is much quicker.

There is a beautiful campsite on Longer Lake, located at the mouth of

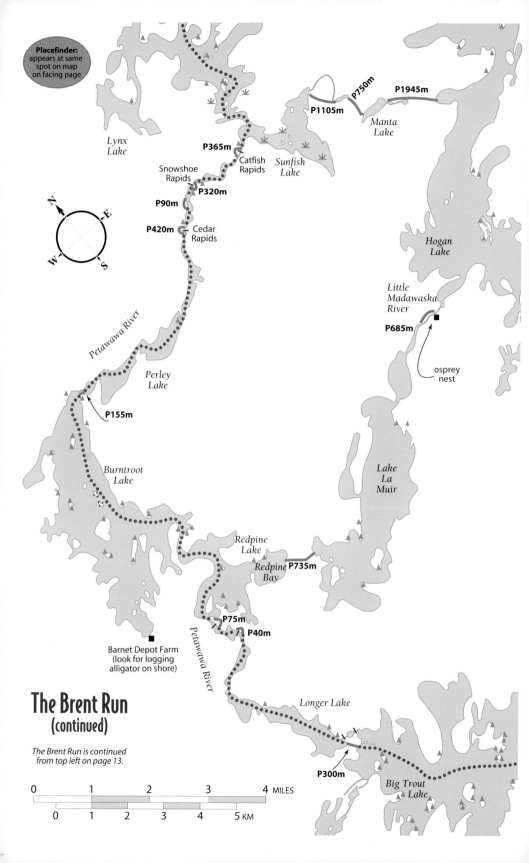

Placefinder:
appears at same
spot on map
on facing page

Lynx
Lake

P1105m

P750m

P1945m

Manta
Lake

P365m

Catfish
Rapids

Sunfish
Lake

Snowshoe
Rapids

P320m

P90m

P420m

Cedar
Rapids

N

E

W

S

Hogan
Lake

Little
Madawaska
River

P685m

Petawawa River

Perley
Lake

osprey
nest

P155m

Burntroot
Lake

Lake
La
Muir

Redpine
Lake

Redpine
Bay

P735m

P75m

P40m

Barnet Depot Farm
(look for logging
alligator on shore)

Petawawa River

Longer Lake

The Brent Run
(continued)

*The Brent Run is continued
from top left on page 13.*

P300m

Big Trout
Lake

0   1   2   3   4 MILES

0   1   2   3   4   5 KM

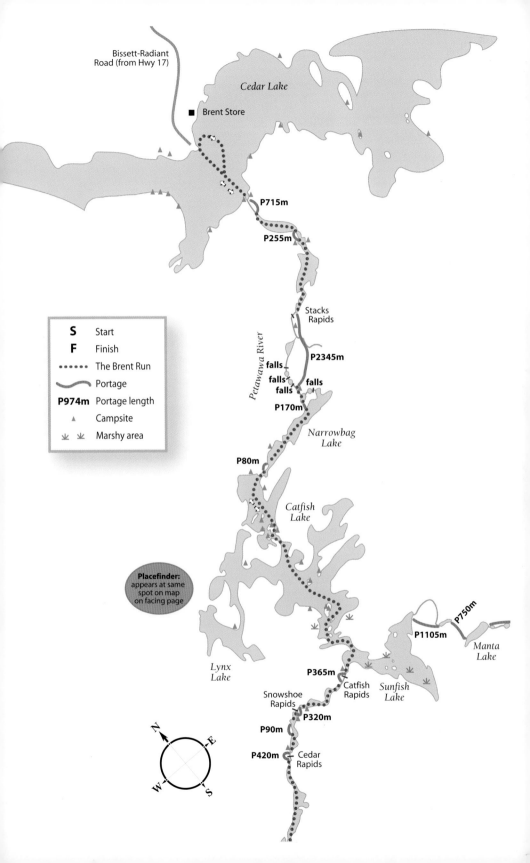

Bissett-Radiant
Road (from Hwy 17)

Cedar Lake

■ Brent Store

P715m

P255m

Stacks
Rapids

Petawawa River

P2345m

falls

falls   falls

falls

P170m

*Narrowbag
Lake*

P80m

*Catfish
Lake*

Placefinder:
appears at same
spot on map
on facing page

*Lynx
Lake*

P750m

P1105m

*Manta
Lake*

P365m

Catfish
Rapids

*Sunfish
Lake*

Snowshoe
Rapids

P320m

P90m

P420m   Cedar
Rapids

S	Start
F	Finish
• • •	The Brent Run
∿	Portage
P974m	Portage length
▲	Campsite
⸽ ⸽	Marshy area

N
E
W
S

The Brent Run

TIME
8 to 10 days

DIFFICULTY
Moderate to
novice

PORTAGES
46

**LONGEST
PORTAGE**
2,565 yards
(2,345 m)

the creek that flows out of the previously mentioned pond; however, it's next to impossible to find it unoccupied. I usually push on to Burntroot by way of two short portages (45 and 80 yards [40 and 75 m]), both marked to the right of a double set of rapids. The second set is an easy swift, but running the first set of rapids is risky. The problem with portaging is that the trail is cluttered with poison ivy; it might be safer to wade or line your canoe down on the right.

The record set for the Brent Run is 23 hours. However, it's better to be a tortoise and not a hare and paddle the route in 8 to 10 days.

From Burntroot, the route heads east down the Petawawa River to Cedar Lake (see Hogan Lake Loop for details). You should arrive on Cedar Lake by late afternoon on your fourth day and still have time to go for a soda and ice cream at the Brent store before making camp.

To return, simply backtrack to Canoe Lake. But when you reach the finish line back at the Portage Store, don't expect a crowd cheering you on from the docks. After all, you've just completed the Brent Run in the worst time in the history of the race. Of course, it's not whether you win or lose, it's what you see along the way that counts!

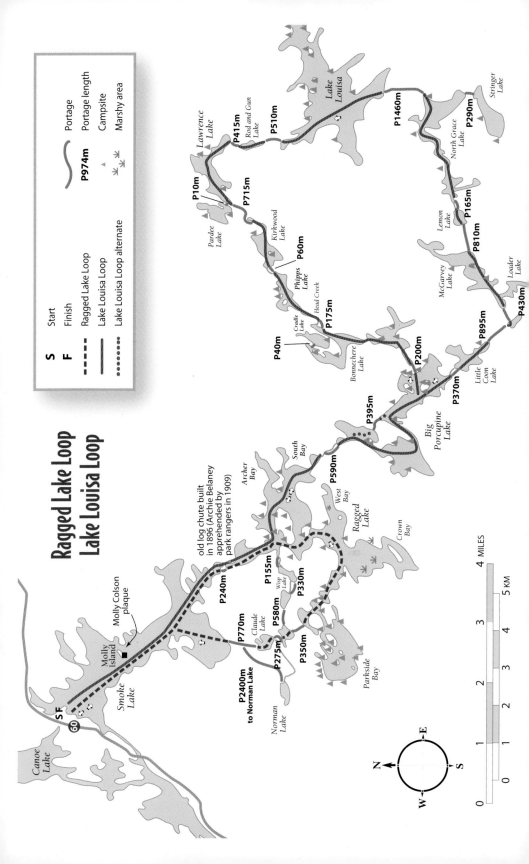

Ragged Lake Loop
Lake Louisa Loop

Legend:

S	Start
F	Finish
– – –	Ragged Lake Loop
——	Lake Louisa Loop
••••	Lake Louisa Loop alternate
◠	Portage
P974m	Portage length
▲	Campsite
🌿	Marshy area

Canoe Lake

Smoke Lake

Molly Island
Molly Colson plaque

old log chute built in 1896 (Archie Belaney apprehended by park rangers in 1909)

P240m
P155m
P770m
Claude Lake
Wisp Lake
P580m
P275m
P2400m to Norman Lake
Norman Lake
P350m
P330m

Archer Bay
South Bay
West Bay
Ragged Lake
Crown Bay
Parkside Bay

P590m
P395m

Big Porcupine Lake
Little Coon Lake
P370m
P200m
P895m
P40m
P175m
Bonnechere Lake
Cradle Lake
Head Creek
Phipps Lake
P60m
Kirkwood Lake
P715m
P10m
Pardee Lake
Lawrence Lake
P415m
Rod and Gun Lake
P510m

Lake Louisa

P1460m
Stringer Lake
P290m
North Grace Lake
P165m
Lemon Lake
P810m
McGarvey Lake
P430m
Loader Lake

N W E S

0 1 2 3 4 MILES
0 1 2 3 4 5 KM

Ragged Lake Loop

ONE OF THE ADVANTAGES OF BEGINNING A TRIP from Smoke Lake rather than its neighbor, Canoe Lake, is that your chance of having a prevailing wind help rather than hinder you is greatly increased. This southern access also offers one of the best weekend circle routes along the Highway 60 corridor — the Ragged Lake loop.

From the launch site, the route heads due south toward Molly Island, named after Molly Cox. Molly was a nurse from Ottawa who came to Algonquin on a holiday to regain her health. She instantly fell in love with the area, with Smoke Lake Island being her favorite picnic site. After marrying Ranger Edwin Colson in 1907, Molly made Algonquin her home.

Together, Molly and Edwin managed the Highland Inn and later took ownership of Hotel Algonquin. But it was her nursing ability that made Molly renowned in the area, and she quickly became known as Algonquin's own Florence Nightingale.

The route continues south on Smoke Lake to the most southern inlet. Here, a 265-yard (240 m) portage heads into Ragged Lake. The original path, nicknamed the Devil's Staircase, worked its way directly uphill and along an old log flume built in 1896. It has since been closed off, and now a somewhat longer but gentler sloping path is marked to the right of the take-out.

Many historical figures have made use of the Smoke Lake/Ragged Lake portage. The first European here was Henry Briscoe, who, in 1826, explored Smoke and Ragged Lakes while looking for a military communication route between Lake Simcoe and the Ottawa River. In 1837, the renowned mapmaker David Thompson also made use of the portage while exploring the Oxtongue and Madawaska Rivers for the possibility of establishing a navigational canal. And after the development of the park itself, rangers con-tinuously used the trail while out on patrol in search of poachers.

One of the most noteworthy poachers in Algonquin was Archie Belaney (Grey Owl). In the winter of 1909, Belaney boasted to another trapper that he could head clear across Algonquin Park undetected by park rangers. It didn't take long for the rangers to catch wind of the bet, and they quickly set out in search of the skilled woodsman, with Mark Robinson and Zeph Naden patrolling from McCraney Lake to the Oxtongue River and Bud Callighen and Albert Ranger patrolling from Cache Lake through Bonnechere Lake to Big Porcupine.

Ragged Lake Loop

TIME
2 to 3 days

DIFFICULTY
Novice

PORTAGES
4

**LONGEST
PORTAGE**
840 yards
(770 m)

There are several reports of Belaney's capture, but the one that seems to ring most true is that of Bud Callighen. In his diary, Callighen writes that long after dark Belaney stumbled into his and Albert's camp. His feet nearly lost to frostbite after falling through thin ice earlier in the night, he asked the rangers for help. Belaney was escorted by all four rangers to park headquarters and was then taken to have his feet treated at Mark Robinson's Canoe Lake shelter hut.

From the put-in of the historic portage, the route choice is yours. Ragged Lake is made up of numerous bays and inlets, with excellent campsites dispersed throughout. Some of the nicest are found just south of the dam, near the large island, and to the far west, in isolated Parkside Bay. I prefer making camp in Parkside Bay simply because it seems more remote from the main lake and is located near the chain of alternative portages that leads back to Smoke Lake.

The first of these portages, measuring 385 yards (350 m) and heading mostly downhill toward an unnamed pond, is just north of the entrance to Parkside Bay. What remains before reaching the southwestern bay of Smoke Lake is a 300-yard (275 m) portage leading into Claude Lake, followed by an 840-yard (770 m) portage taking you out.

Lake Louisa Loop

SMOKE LAKE IS AN EXCELLENT STARTING POINT FOR a canoe loop to Lake Louisa, which is considered one of the more scenic lakes in the south end. The route begins by heading south to Ragged Lake over a 265-yard (240 m) portage. Continue south on Ragged Lake toward the 645-yard (590 m) portage into Big Porcupine Lake.

While exiting Ragged Lake's northern outlet, be sure not to confuse the large island in the center of the lake as the mainland. In doing this, many canoeists go to the right of the island and end up heading southwest into Crown Bay. If you simply keep to the left once out of the inlet and then paddle directly south, you'll eventually reach the shallow bay and the take-out for the Big Porcupine Lake portage.

The Porcupine Lake portage, running along the right-hand side of a small stream, is short, but extremely steep. Fortunately, the park staff has erected a number of canoe rests along the way.

I'll never forget my first trip along this grueling portage. Alana and I, while returning down the hill for our second load, came upon a group of youths loaded down with heavy traditional canvas packs. Just as we were passing them, one of the smaller boys, named Josh, suddenly keeled over backward onto his pack. After spotting poor Josh kicking away like an over-turned turtle, we stopped to lend him a hand. Once we got the youngster back on his feet, he thanked us profusely, shook the dirt off his hands, strapped his heavy load back on, and then, oddly, stated, "Ya know, that pack's heavier than a penguin."

Big Porcupine Lake has two distinct halves: the north arm and south arm. Directly across from the put-in of the previous portage is a 430-yard (395 m) portage that joins both sections. But I find it a lot simpler just to paddle around the lake and through the shallow narrows to reach the south end. Both sections offer an excellent choice of campsites, making Porcupine Lake a perfect spot to spend your first night.

The loop begins from Big Porcupine Lake's southernmost end, and heads over the 405-yard (370 m) portage into Little Coon Lake. From there, continue south into Whatnot Lake by way of an 980-yard (895 m) portage complete with the roughest take-out of the entire trip.

Whatnot Lake is nothing more than a muddy pond with an unbearable stench, and during low water levels the paddle across to the 470-yard (430 m) portage leading into McGarvey Lake can become quite a challenge.

Alana's secret recipe — Eggplant Parmesan.

Once in McGarvey, however, the trip becomes less difficult. Keep to the right shoreline, and once you've passed the island three-quarters of the way across, follow the 885-yard (810 m) portage into the shallow waters of Lemon Lake.

What remains before making camp for your second night are a 180-yard (165 m) portage from Lemon Lake to North Grace, and a 1,600-yard (1,460 m) portage into Louisa itself. The last portage of the day also happens to be the longest en route, but by traveling the loop in a counter-clockwise direction, the majority of the trail leads downhill.

On the third day of the trip, travel north out of Lake Louisa by way of the extremely steep but downward 560-yard (510 m) portage into Rod and Gun Lake and the 455-yard (415 m) portage into Lawrence Lake.

Then, from the west end of Lawrence, head west into Kirkwood Lake. Note that the 780-yard (715 m) portage is shared at first by a short portage leading to Pardee Lake.

At the end of the Kirkwood portage, you have the choice of two put-ins. (Your decision will depend on the water level.) Then, after making your way along a shallow, sand-bottomed creek and across to the west end of Kirkwood Lake, a 65-yard (60 m) lift-over to the left of a small cascade will take you into Phipps Lake.

For the last few hundred yards of Phipps Lake, a weedy, twisting creek must be paddled to reach the next portage (190 yards [175 m]). After you have crossed into Bonnechere Pond and Bonnechere Lake, a final 220-yard (200 m) portage marked at the end of Bonnechere Lake's southwest bay takes you back to Big Porcupine Lake. The loop ends here, and the rest of the route simply retraces itself.

Even though I usually spend my first night camped on Big Porcupine, my preference is to stay there for the last night as well, especially if it's at the end of the summer season, when the loons are gathering on the lake before heading south.

I remember on one particular trip I was paddling between the two central islands and counted a total of twenty-eight loons — screaming, splashing, racing in circles on the surface of the water, and then taxiing across to the opposite end of the lake. At dusk, I sat on a rocky point at my campsite and listened to their mournful calls; the unvaried tone was almost wolf-like. Come mid-September, the call of the loon is the predominant sound during a still night out on Big Porcupine Lake.

For five thousand years, Natives have revered the loon as a sacred bird, believing that its call was a bridge between the material and spiritual worlds. The Cree believed the call to be that of a dead warrior who was forbidden entry to Heaven, and Chipewyans considered it an omen of death.

Lake Louisa Loop

TIME
4 to 5 days

DIFFICULTY
Moderate to novice

PORTAGES
16

LONGEST PORTAGE
1,600 yards (1,460 m)

Perfect island campsite on Catfish Lake

Hogan Lake Loop

AFTER DRIVING THE DUSTY, WASHBOARD ROAD LEADING INTO Brent, you'd think that town residents would want the park staff to fix it up a bit to boost business. But according to Jake Pigeon, the operator of the Brent store, "If they fill in all those pot holes, all the riffraff would come driving in and the canoeing up here would be the shits!"

He's right. The Brent access on Cedar Lake still offers a number of prime, almost riffraff-free canoe trips, unlike most of the access points along the well-maintained Highway 60 corridor. The Hogan Lake loop happens to be one of Jake's favorites.

To reach the remote access point, turn south off Highway 17 onto Bissett-Radiant Road, just west of Deux Rivières. Drive for 10 miles (16 km) to the park gatehouse, at the fork in the road. You must pick up your interior camping permit here before continuing to the right for another 15 miles (24 km). The put-in is on the opposite side of the tracks, before Brent's main street. If you plan on arriving late in the day, you can use the campground adjacent to the access point.

The first day out is the hardest going. From the docks at the put-in, the route heads directly across Cedar Lake to a 780-yard (715 m) portage marked to the left of where the Petawawa River empties out into the lake. Halfway along, the trail heads up two short hills and then forks. The side trail to the right leads to a dramatic waterfall, but the main portage continues to the left, ending just past a wooden cross that marks the gravesite of A. Corbeil, a logger who drowned at the base of the cascade while on a log drive in June 1888.

After a short paddle up a wide, weedy stretch of the river, another portage leads around another set of falls. The steep, 280-yard (255 m) trail works its way to the right of the scenic cascade. The view is spectacular, but upstream there is an even more impressive stretch of white water called Stacks Rapids. A 2,565-yard (2,345 m) portage — the longest en route — is marked to the left at the base of the rapids.

The river twists to the left, tucking itself under a low wooden bridge and into Narrowbag Lake. Your route to the lake, however, is somewhat different. From the put-in of the 2,565-yard (2,345 m) portage, head directly across into a large back bay. Then, following the left-hand shoreline, locate the marked portage (185 yards [170 m]) leading up and over a timber-covered hill.

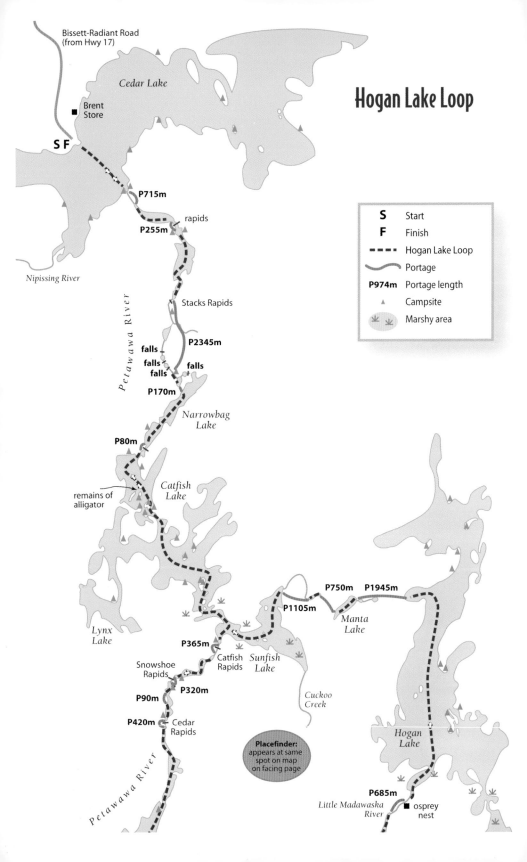

Hogan Lake Loop

Bissett-Radiant Road
(from Hwy 17)

Cedar Lake

Brent
Store

S F

P715m

rapids

P255m

Nipissing River

Petawawa River

Stacks Rapids

P2345m

falls
falls   falls
falls

P170m

Narrowbag Lake

P80m

remains of
alligator

Catfish Lake

P750m   **P1945m**

P1105m

Manta Lake

Lynx Lake

P365m

Catfish
Rapids

Sunfish Lake

Snowshoe
Rapids

Cuckoo Creek

P90m   **P320m**

P420m   Cedar
Rapids

Placefinder:
appears at same
spot on map
on facing page

Hogan Lake

Petawawa River

P685m

Little Madawaska River

osprey
nest

S	Start
F	Finish
- - -	Hogan Lake Loop
⌇	Portage
P974m	Portage length
▲	Campsite
🌿 🌿	Marshy area

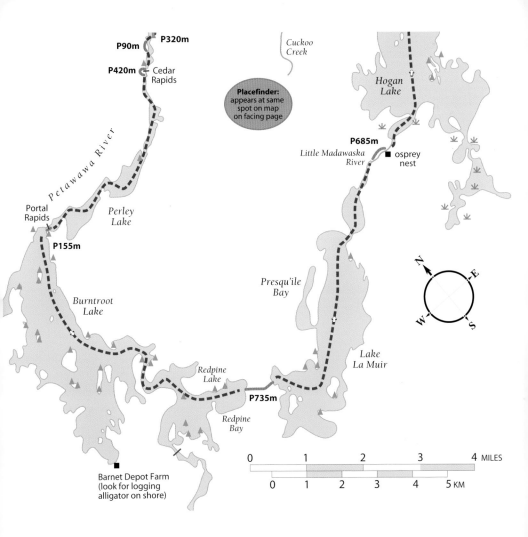

At the far end of Narrowbag — a rather inelegant name that does no justice to this pretty lake — is the last portage of the day, leading into Catfish Lake. The take-out of the 90-yard (80 m) trail is marked to the right of a swift littered with debris left behind from past log drives. A much more impressive logging artifact than the half-decayed log chute, however, is Catfish Lake's marooned alligator, located on the second of three islands clustered together at the north end.

Invented by John Ceburn West in 1889, the alligator was a powerful steam-driven tug capable of dragging booms of up to sixty thousand logs for ten hours on less than a cord of wood. It also had the unique ability to winch itself overland.

One of the park's first ranger cabins was built at the headwaters of Catfish Lake. (I'm uncertain of its exact location.) Here, Ranger Joseph Gauthier — the grand old man of Catfish Lake — made use of the cabin while on his

beat from Cedar Lake to Burntroot. The ranger was known for not being able to speak or write a word of English, and he would have to ask passing canoeists to translate his French into his daily journal.

Both the upper and lower sections of Catfish Lake have excellent campsites. My preference, however, is the lower section, with my favorite site being directly east of the central island and south of Turtle Rock (a high rock ledge where Natives once came to worship).

An upstream battle on the Petawawa continues the next day, beginning at the marshy south end of Catfish Lake. Soon, a short paddle against the slow-moving current, which gurgles past cedar-lined banks and clumps of

*Peregrine falcons once nested on the cliffs
lining the shoreline of Hogan Lake*

sedge, brings you to where Cuckoo Creek empties out of Sunfish Lake, to
the south. Here, the loop portion of the route begins.

It's best to travel in a counterclockwise direction here, remaining on the
Petawawa and heading up toward Burntroot Lake. But just upstream from
where the small tributary flows in from the south you'll find a number of
rapids.

The first is Catfish Rapids, with a 400-yard (365 m) portage marked
to the right, followed shortly after by Snowshoe rapids, with a shorter,
350-yard (320 m) portage marked to the left. After Snowshoe Rapids, past
the marked portage into North Cuckoo Lake, is a small unnamed rapid

Portaging is necessary at times (Petawawa River).

with a 100-yard (90 m) portage to the right. It may be possible to avoid this portage altogether and simply pole your canoe up the quick swift.

The last obstacle in this series of white water is Cedar Rapids. The flat but rocky portage (460 yards [420 m]) is marked to the right and heads into long, narrow Perley Lake.

What remains before you make camp on Burntroot Lake, a lake randomly dotted with island campsites, is a 3-mile (5 km) paddle across Perley Lake and a quick, 170-yard (155 m) portage marked to the left of Portal Rapids (named after Lord Portal, a wartime marshal of the Royal Air Force, who visited the lake on a fishing trip in 1946).

For a time, between 1964 and 1973, Burntroot Lake was also called Portal Lake. It eventually went back to its original title, derived from both Joseph Bouchette's 1846 map of Upper Canada, upon which the lake was labeled Burnt Lake, and Dickson's 1886 account of an extensive burn site along a hillside to the north. The name was changed to Burntroot in 1931, however, to help distinguish it from Burnt Island Lake to the south.

The second day is somewhat shorter than the first, and you'll probably make camp on Burntroot Lake by mid-afternoon, giving you ample time to paddle down to the far end of the southwestern bay and explore the site of the Barnet Depot Farm. Not much remains of the original buildings, first occupied back in 1882 to keep a fresh supply of produce available for the neighboring logging camps. But an alligator, much more intact than the tug left out on Catfish Lake, rests up along the shoreline here.

Your destination for day three is Hogan Lake, to the east. The route leaves Burntroot, heading southeast, all the way down into Red-pine Bay. Here, an 805-yard (735 m) portage works itself over a steep rise and into picturesque Lake La Muir.

Surprisingly, it's the Lake La Muir portage that's usually the most crowded. During my last trip into Lake La Muir, I met up with a couple of canoeists who had burdened themselves with someone else's pack, which was left behind at the other end of the portage. It was an old canvas pack filled with a beat-up tarp, a clump of wet cloths and a bag of assorted garbage. The ethical canoeists caught up to the owners of the pack, and thinking they had simply forgotten it, gave the pack back to them. But the unthankful degenerates threw the pack to the ground, cursed at the couple, and quickly left the scene.

Many unprincipled canoeists, finding themselves overloaded along the portage, end up leaving their surplus behind. During a one-year period of canoeing in Algonquin, I came across an incredible assortment of leftovers: thirty-seven socks, half a dozen sneakers, five lawn chairs, four PFDs, three foam footballs, two perfectly good sleeping bags, two coolers chewed apart by bears, and a brand-new Tilley hat. Some of the gear I packed out with me — the hat was a perfect fit — but the rest of the stuff I had to leave behind.

Once on Lake La Muir, keep close to the north shore and paddle east toward the weedy shallows where the Little Madawaska begins. The waterway is lined with fallen dead cedar along most of its length, and just before a 750-yard (685 m) portage to the left of where the river drops over a rock shelf is an active osprey nest.

The osprey, more commonly known as a "fish hawk," is known for returning to the same nest year after year, sometimes for generations. The female lays her eggs in late April, or May, and, while she stays with the young for the first month, the male is busy trying to catch enough fish to feed the entire family. After the birds migrate in late September, however, the young stay south for two years before returning to Ontario.

From the muddy put-in of the 750-yard (685 m) portage, the narrow river twists itself through a cat-tail marsh and then flushes out into Hogan Lake. Hogan is one of Algonquin's natural wonders. Forested hills crowd the shoreline, and an extensive marshland to the south hosts countless

Hogan Lake Loop

TIME
5 days

DIFFICULTY
Moderate

PORTAGES
20

LONGEST PORTAGE
2,565 yards
(2,345 m)

moose sightings. Peregrine falcons have even been sighted recently, nesting on an impressive granite wall to the east of the first large island. The wilderness appeal of the large lake is enhanced by a surprising lack of campsites (of course, this may not be such an appealing attribute if you arrive at the lake late in the day and find all the sites occupied).

After enjoying a night of seclusion, travel north back toward Catfish Lake. The first portage (2,130 yards [1,945 m]), located in a bay three-quarters of the way along the lake, is a rough trail, especially halfway along, where you have to clamber up a steep incline. At the crest of the hill, note the countless bear-claw marks left on the thin, seamless bark of the beech trees. These wounds are made when the bear shimmies up the trunk to get at the crop of beechnuts. If you take a closer look, you might see a "bear nest" in the crotch of the tree, where the bruin pulls in branches while feeding, breaking the limbs as they gorge.

After a short paddle across Manta Lake, you'll come to another portage (820 yards [750 m]), marked to the right of a small creek. It is flatter than the previous portage, but because of the lack of trail maintenance in the area lately, it can be just as rough.

Only a trip across the pond-like Newt Lake and an easy 1,210-yard (1,105 m) portage beginning under a giant white pine remain. A downward slope marks the end of the portage and the entrance to Sunfish Lake.

Two channels are marked to the west on Sunfish Lake. Take the one to the right, and work your way through the swampy maze back to the Petawawa River. The loop ends here, and it's a short paddle downstream to Catfish Lake, where you'll spend your last night out.

The next day it's downstream all the way from Catfish to Cedar. Of course, you'll have to endure the same lengthy portages you had to contend with on your first day out, as well as the long, bumpy drive back to the highway.

Dividing Lake

TUCKED AWAY ALONG THE FRINGE OF ALGONQUIN'S SOUTHWEST border is the Dividing Lake Nature Reserve, a natural museum of century-old pine scattered through a stand of mature hardwood. Even though an arduous portage — known locally as the Golden Staircase — stands in your way, a visit to witness Algonquin's protected natural landscape is well worth the effort.

To reach the access point, drive along Highway 35 to Dorset. Just north of the town, turn right onto Kawagama Lake Road 8 (your permit can be picked up at Tower Hill Marina on Highway 35, just before the Kawagama Lake Road turn-off). Follow the paved road for almost half a mile (0.7 km) to the second junction, turn right and continue for 15 miles (23.6 km) to the road leading to Livingston Lake Lodge. Also, be sure not to leave your vehicle parked at the lodge: the management will have it towed. Park on the right side of the road as it bends to the left, away from the lake.

A quick paddle down Livingstone Lake will bring you to the first portage. The 250-yard (230 m) trail is marked to the right of a government dam and leads into Bear Lake. Paddle to the far end of Bear Lake and take the shallow channel to the left into Kimball Lake. If water levels are low, you may have to make use of a second, 350-yard (320 m) portage marked to the right, upstream from a beaver dam.

The Golden Staircase, measuring 3,000 yards (2,745 m), begins on the far end of Kimball Lake. At first, the trail works its way through a wet, bug-infested lowland; it then veers north up a steep grade alongside a cascading falls and ends at Rockaway Lake.

I'll never forget taking on this extensive portage a few years back. I felt a bad cold coming on the day before the trip, but after taking a heavy dose of extra-strength Neo Citran I was able to convince my canoeing companions that I was still fit enough to tag along. By the time I reached the halfway point on the Rockaway Lake portage, however, my chest cold began to resemble pneumonia. But I had carried over long and steep portages before, and even with a hacking cough draining my energy, I persuaded myself that I could get through it again.

It was just after 6 p.m. by the time we completed the portage and paddled to the end of Rockaway Lake to make camp on the border of the forest reserve. In minutes I erected my tent, unrolled my sleeping bag, and began

Dividing Lake

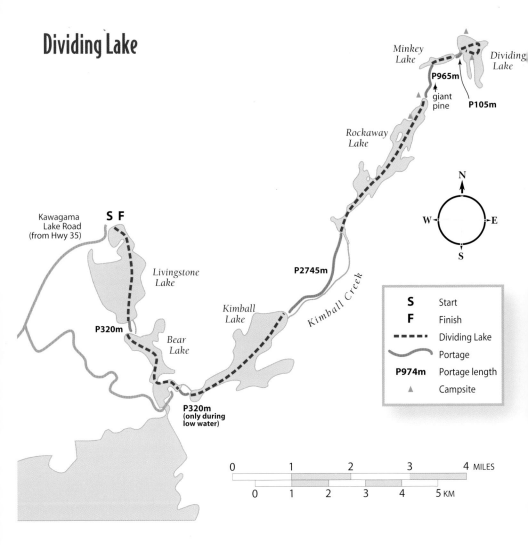

to boil chicken noodle soup. After a generous amount of Tylenol and a cup of hot tea, I went straight to bed.

A chilling frost visited camp that night, freezing the water bottles and leaving me with a high fever. By morning my cold was so bad that I feared for my long-term health. While my canoemates took the day to portage and paddle into Dividing Lake to fish for speckled trout, taking the 1,055-yard (965 m) portage into Minkey Lake and a 115-yard (105 m) portage into Dividing Lake, I spent the day in camp fighting my fever. I transformed my tent into a sweat hut, and spent a couple of hours leaning over steaming rocks. By mid-afternoon my fever began to break. With a clear head and nose, I decided to walk back into the bush beyond our campsite to visit the giant white pines on the portage between Minkey and Dividing Lake.

There, among equally impressive hemlock and yellow birch, stood the lonely monarchs of the forest. How these few gigantic pines managed to hide from the loggers of the past I have no idea. Perhaps the rugged terrain that we had to struggle across to reach the trees is what saved them. Two hundred years old and 150 feet (50 m) high, the trees are so broad at their trunks that three people cannot reach around them. As I viewed the scant remains of Ontario's primeval wilderness, my fever mysteriously vanished.

We eventually made it back to the Livingstone Lake access (via the same route), and I ended up pushing penicillin for a week, cursing myself for not having been smart enough to cancel the canoe trip when I had the chance.

Dividing Lake

TIME
2 to 3 days

DIFFICULTY
Except for a good bill of health to help you along the steep, 3,000–yard (2,745 m) portage, only novice tripping experience is needed.

PORTAGES
8

LONGEST PORTAGE
3,000 yards (2,745 m)

Solo tripping can become extremely addictive (Lake Louisa).

Rock Lake

THINKING BACK, I GUESS IT'S MONICA, THE CUTE blonde who sat in front of me in history class, I have to thank for introducing me to Rock Lake. You see, back in high school my friends were organizing a couples' weekend to Algonquin's Rock Lake Campground. It took days of begging and pleading with my parents just to get permission to go. But that was the easy part; I still had to get up enough nerve to ask Monica to be my date. I finally whispered my proposal to her between note taking on the Russian Revolution, and she, in turn, blurted out, "You're kidding, right?"

Of course, my friends tried to console me by asking me to come along anyway, and I was foolish enough to say yes. It didn't take long after we arrived at the campground, however, to notice that my idea of a good time didn't necessarily jibe with that of the rest of the group; so I did what any distraught bachelor would do while camping with a bunch of love-struck teenagers — I went solo. For years after, I returned on the same long weekend to embark on countless solo trips. The following are five of my favorites.

The first is an interior trip on Rock Lake, which park regulars have labeled Algonquin's "southern gem." This lake was named by John Snow during his survey of the Madawaska River in 1854. He was obviously impressed with the perpendicular rock that towered over 300 feet (100 m) above the waters of the eastern shoreline.

To access the Rock Lake put-in, turn south off Highway 60 onto the gravel road leading to the Rock Lake Campground. Five miles (8 km) later you will come to a crossroads. The put-in is straight ahead, but first you must turn left and drive to the gatehouse to obtain your interior camping permit.

From the docks at the access point, the route heads left, down the short stretch of the Madawaska River, and out into Rock Lake. The north end of the lake is cluttered, with a busy campground and a number of cottage sites, but the designated interior campsites are located to the south, the best being situated on two of the three large islands and also near the base of a rock wall. The rare peregrine falcon once called this and other surrounding rock ridges home, until the species was almost totally eradicated by DDT in the early 1960s. In fact, Rock Lake was once called Falcon Lake, as recorded by mapmaker David Thompson in 1837.

Rock Lake is an excellent place for the history buff. Along the east shore, on a large point halfway down the lake, are the remains of the Barclay

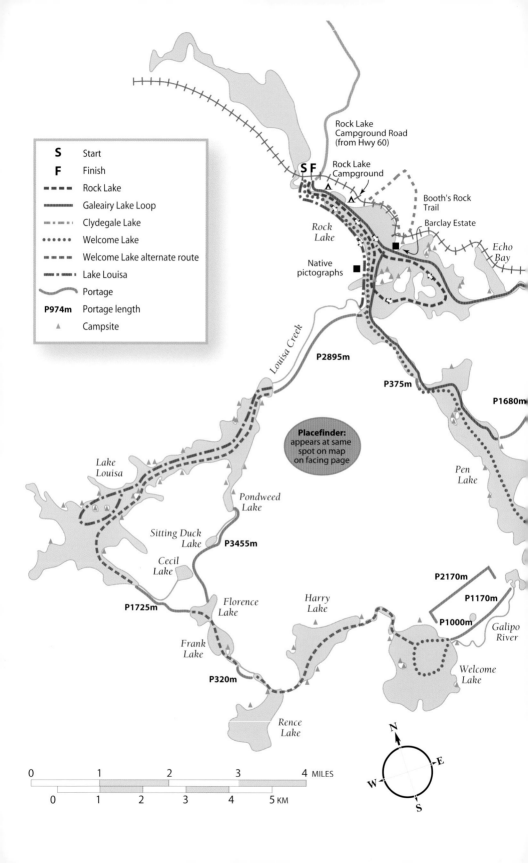

S Start
F Finish
- - - Rock Lake
━━━ Galeairy Lake Loop
-·-·- Clydegale Lake
••••• Welcome Lake
- - - Welcome Lake alternate route
-··-··- Lake Louisa
⌇⌇⌇ Portage
P974m Portage length
▲ Campsite

Rock Lake
Campground Road
(from Hwy 60)

Rock Lake
Campground

Booth's Rock
Trail

Barclay Estate

Echo
Bay

Rock
Lake

Native
pictographs

P2895m

Louisa Creek

P375m

P1680m

Placefinder:
appears at same
spot on map
on facing page

Pen
Lake

Lake
Louisa

Pondweed
Lake

Sitting Duck
Lake

P3455m

Cecil
Lake

P2170m

P1170m

P1000m

Galipo
River

P1725m

Florence
Lake

Harry
Lake

Frank
Lake

Welcome
Lake

P320m

Rence
Lake

0   1   2   3   4 MILES

0   1   2   3   4   5 KM

N
E
W
S

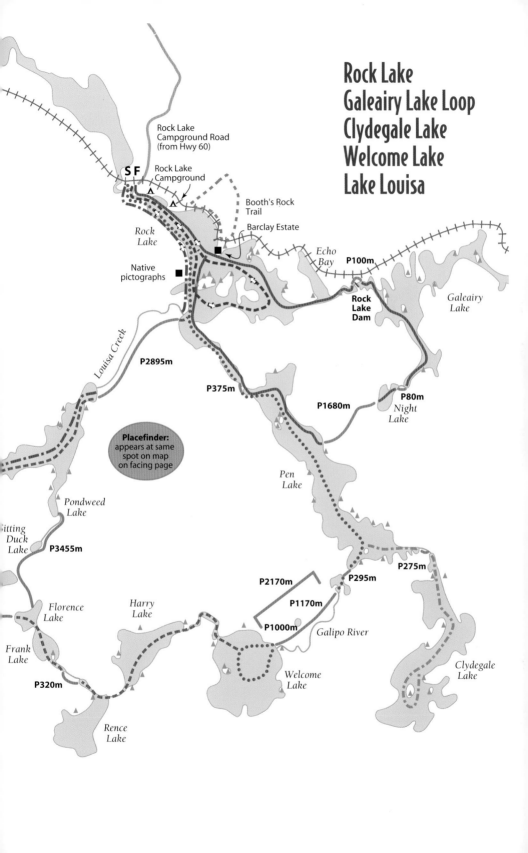

Rock Lake
Galeairy Lake Loop
Clydegale Lake
Welcome Lake
Lake Louisa

Rock Lake
Campground Road
(from Hwy 60)

S F

Rock Lake
Campground

Booth's Rock
Trail

Barclay Estate

*Rock
Lake*

Echo
Bay

P100m

Native
pictographs

Rock
Lake
Dam

*Galeairy
Lake*

Louisa Creek

P2895m

P375m

P1680m

P80m
*Night
Lake*

Placefinder:
appears at same
spot on map
on facing page

*Pen
Lake*

*Pondweed
Lake*

P275m

*Sitting
Duck
Lake*

P3455m

P2170m

P295m

P1170m

*Florence
Lake*

*Harry
Lake*

P1000m

Galipo River

*Clydegale
Lake*

*Frank
Lake*

*Welcome
Lake*

P320m

*Rence
Lake*

Rock Lake's Native pictograph site.

Estate. This once-immaculate property was owned by Judge George Barclay, a relative of the well-known lumber baron J. R. Booth, and was last occupied in the summer of 1953. The historic site is slowly being taken over by the surrounding forest, and all that's left are the well-defined remnants of the tennis court, dock and foundations.

From the grounds of the Barclay Estate you can hook up to the 3-mile (5 km) Booth's Rock Trail and hike up to the clifftop for a view of Rock Lake, and Whitefish Lake to the north.

On the opposite shore, canoeists can observe Native pictographs — one of the few remaining signs of the park's earlier inhabitants. The rock paintings are believed to be by neighboring Ojibwa from the west. The Ojibwa frequently traveled through the area after they helped the Algonquin tribes chase out the Iroquois — their long-time adversaries — in the late 1600s. To locate the site, paddle to the north side of the bay, almost directly across from the west point of Jean Island. The pictographs, consisting of the vague traces of animals and a few tally marks, are on a wedge of rock close to the water's edge. The red ochre having faded over time, the paintings have become difficult to see against the pink granite.

The second route exits Rock Lake at its most southeastern inlet and heads into Galeairy Lake by way of a 110-yard (100 m) portage to the left of a cement dam.

Galeairy Lake, its tranquil waters lined with cedar and hemlock, has nice campsites, and an abandoned railway line along its eastern shore makes an excellent hiking trail. The track was constructed in 1890 under the direction of J. R. Booth, and stretched from Ottawa to Georgian Bay. Although it was the busiest railway in Canada during the First World War, the line was later abandoned in 1944.

After spending a night on Galeairy Lake, you can either backtrack to Rock Lake or circle back by way of Pen Lake. If you choose the latter, paddle south, down to the far end of Galeairy's narrow inlet. From here, make a right and carry over the 90-yard (80 m) portage into Night Lake. It's a quick paddle across Night Lake — more a weedy pond than a lake — to where the long, but flat 1,840-yard (1,680 m) portage leads into Pen Lake.

To complete the loop, on your last day, head north on Pen Lake and squeeze to the right of the two islands blocking the route (the more direct route through the center channel is usually too shallow to paddle without scraping up your paint job). Then, from the top end of Pen Lake, an easy, 410-yard (375 m) portage, to the left of a historic logging chute and a scenic cascade, takes you into Rock Lake's southwestern inlet, leaving an hour's paddle back to the access point.

The third route follows the right-hand shoreline of Rock Lake. You reach Pen Lake by way of the 410-yard (375 m) portage. It then takes you to the extreme south end of Pen, to a 300-yard (275 m) portage into Clydegale Lake. Except for a rough take-out, the portage, marked to the right of another section of fast water, is worth the extra effort. Clydegale is not as well used as Pen, so wildlife sightings are far more numerous. I camped at the lake's southern end and was visited by a family of curious otters, a grouping of twelve loons, three moose, and a deer that swam across the lake and dragged itself out of the water just a few yards from my tent.

*Spring fever along the shores of Lake Louisa
(male and female mergansers).*

The return trip is via the same route, but with the prevailing winds against you on your way back, make sure you leave for Rock Lake early.

The fourth trip is to Welcome Lake, and happens to be the most challenging but also the most rewarding of the five routes. To reach Welcome Lake, follow route three, and, instead of heading south into Clydegale, take the series of portages along Galipo River, which flows into Pen Lake from the west.

To locate the first portage, paddle into the weedy bay to the right of a knob-topped island covered in stout pine. The first portage (325 yards

[295 m]) climbs up to the left of a beautiful waterfall and ends at the swampy expanse of Galipo River.

The river is more of a weedy creek than a major waterway, and it's a quick paddle from the put-in and up the twisting channel to the next set of portages. Here, the older Algonquin maps indicate a 1,280-yard (1,170 m) portage into a small pond, followed by a 1,095-yard (1000 m) portage into Welcome Lake. In reality, the pond is now almost totally dry and the two trails have become one long 2,375-yard (2170 m) portage.

The long haul to Welcome Lake is worth all the sweat and strain. The circular lake is adorned with prime beach sites, and its remote setting offers some of the best brook-trout fishing in the park. The only drawbacks are the odd leech cruising the sandy shoreline and the strict fishing regulations that the MNR has been forced to place on the lake to help save the natural genetic strain of trout.

Of Algonquin's brook-trout lakes, formed after the glaciers retreated some ten thousand years ago, 230 contain fish with hatchery-marked genes, and only nineteen have pure native strains. These native strains have been labeled "heritage fish." They have slower growth and maturation rates than stocked fish and are also much better adapted to dealing with the harsh, changing environments characteristic of Algonquin's deep, cold lakes.

Along with the hardship of coping with the lake's adverse conditions, Algonquin's brook trout also have to deal with some fifty thousand anglers that visit the park every year. On Welcome Lake, the MNR enforces a daily possession limit of two fish per person, a minimum size limit of 14 inches (36 cm), and a total ban on bait. Some lakes in the more central interior of Algonquin have been designated as voluntary catch-and-release lakes, and nearby Stringer Lake has been closed for fishing altogether.

Once on Welcome Lake, you can either spend the second day exploring Harry and Rence Lakes, to the northwest, and then backtrack to Rock Lake on day three, or, using the remaining two days, take on an even more adventurous return trip by way of Lake Louisa.

To reach Louisa from Welcome Lake, continue up the Galipo River into Harry and then Rence Lake. Almost immediately after the entrance to Rence, head north up another shallow stream and a muddy 350-yard (320 m) portage into the connected Frank and Florence Lakes.

Two portages connect Florence Lake to Lake Louisa. If the pre-vailing winds are extreme, you can choose to take the 3,780-yard (3,455 m) path located at the northeast corner of Florence Lake. This will allow you to avoid paddling almost the entire length of Lake Louisa. But the shorter,

Rock Lake

TIME
Five routes
ranging from
2 to 4 days

DIFFICULTY
Except for the
Lake Louisa
loop, only
novice tripping
experience is
needed.

PORTAGES
Five routes
ranging from
0 to 6 portages

**LONGEST
PORTAGE**
3,165 yards
(2,895 m)
Lake Louisa
route

1,885-yard (1,725 m) path at the northwest corner is a better-maintained trail and a more direct route; just be sure not to get lost where the portage joins up with a logging road approximately 110 yards (100 m) from the put-in. Turn right onto the road. Then, after about a two-minute walk, turn left back into the bush. It may seem straightforward, but with a canoe balanced over your head it's easy to miss the turnoff and continue blindly down the road.

What remains the next day is an hour-and-a-half paddle to the east end of Louisa, followed by a 3,165-yard (2,895 m) portage into Rock Lake. The portage begins to the right of a giant logjam, and, like the previous portage, makes use of a logging road. It then follows an old tote road that is now almost totally obscured under a dark canopy of mixed hardwoods.

The fifth and last of my proposed three-day canoe routes from the Rock Lake access point is a straight carry into Lake Louisa by way of the previously mentioned 3,165-yard (2,895 m) portage. Paddle down Rock Lake, hugging the right shoreline, until you reach the take-out, shortly after the Native pictograph site.

Even though the Rock Lake access point provides the easiest and fastest way to explore Lake Louisa, there is no question that the portage is a long hike (a one-way trip takes about forty minutes). To make matters worse, you also have to backtrack on the same portage during your return trip.

Rosebary Lake Loop

TRAVELING ANY OF THE LOW-MAINTENANCE AREAS — INDICATED by black lines on the park's canoe map — is always a gamble. But during early spring, when the water levels are up and the season's blackfly population has yet to hatch, safe passage can be had. So, when my wife's brother, Aaron, visited us from Prince Edward Island in mid-May and asked me to take him on his first canoe trip, I thought Algonquin's Rosebary Lake loop would be perfect. Who would have guessed that the water level would be at a record low this year, or that, by some cruel act of Mother Nature, the insects would hatch a good two weeks early?

The route begins on the Tim River, just one-and-a-half miles (2 km) upstream of Tim Lake. To reach the access point, follow the directions for the Magnetawan Lake access (see Chapter 16), except three-quarters of a mile (1 km) past the permit office turn left at the fork and follow the road for approximately 3 miles (5 km) to the parking lot alongside the river. The put-in is to the right of the bridge, and a twenty-minute paddle downstream will take you to Tim Lake.

To travel the loop in a clockwise direction, paddle to the north end of Tim Lake's large central island. The first portage is marked directly across from the island and heads into Chibiabos Lake. The 380-yard (345 m) trail is muddy in sections and has a steep incline, but is not a bad carry overall.

The next portage (350 yards [320 m]) is hidden up in the northeast bay of Chibiabos Lake. The take-out is to the right of a shallow stream. During high water levels it is possible to paddle farther along the creek to a second take-out. The first trail, however, is more direct. Near the put-in, the portage crosses a logging road and heads down a steep grade to Indian Pipe Lake.

From the northwest tip of Indian Pipe, the route continues along a 900-yard (820 m) portage leading into West Koko Pond, followed by a 865-yard (790 m) portage into Big Bob Lake. Both portages head over stunted knolls carpeted in moose maple and beech trees and the lower, soggy sections are decorated with lime-green tamarack and rare patches of pink lady's-slipper.

The portage to the Nipissing River, marked to the left of a small creek, is a short paddle across from the put-in at Big Bob Lake. But before making the 220-yard (200 m) carry to the muddy banks of the river, take advantage of the lake's rocky shoreline, where a good breeze will help to ensure a bug-free lunch.

Rosebary Lake Loop

S Start
F Finish
Rosebary Lake Loop
Portage
P974m Portage length
▲ Campsite
↯ Marshy area

Nipissing River

Loontail Creek

P845m

Latour Creek

P1370m

Floating Heart Lake

P365m

Longbow Lake

Rosebary Lake

Grass Lake

P240m

Little Butt Lake

Nipissing River

P100m

P200m

rapids

P55m

Tim River

P120m

rapids

P65m

dam

P65m

Indian Pipe Lake

P320m

West Koko Pond

Chibiabos Lake

P820m

P345m

Tim Lake

P200m

P790m

Big Bob Lake

N
E
S
W

S F
(right side of bridge)

0 1 2 3 4 MILES

0 1 2 3 4 5 KM

The Nipissing is typical of most rivers in Algonquin's western watershed — a gentle current, bordered by marsh grass and shrubs. But at this portion of the river, the swampy shoreline seems even more incessant. Even the last quarter of the trail is over tussocks of marsh grass, and to reach the put-in without sinking up to our hips, Aaron and I had to balance on top of the dry mounds of dirt.

Three miles (2 km) downstream from the put-in, the riverbanks finally squeeze through a section of rock. Two portages, both 70 yards (60 m) in length, follow in quick succession here, the first being marked to the left and the second to the right. Shortly after, another portage (60 yards [55 m]) works its way around a stunted cascade. The trail is on the left bank, and comes equipped with an adequate campsite.

The next two portages, approximately forty minutes from the falls, are slightly longer than the previous ones. The first, marked to the right, measures 220 yards (200 m) and passes over a small hill. The second, marked to the left, is 110 yards (100 m) and is relatively flat.

It was around 4 p.m. when Aaron and I reached this stretch of the river, and eager to try our luck for brook trout at the rapids, we dropped our gear at a campsite located halfway along the first portage and sneaked up to the deep pool at the base of a rock ledge. Five minutes later, the only thing biting was the horde of blackflies that had zoomed in on us. We ran back up to grab our packs and escaped downriver to look for a more bug-free spot to spend the night.

A short distance downriver, the shoreline disappears behind a wall of thick alder bushes, a haven for more bloodthirsty insects. We pushed and pulled our canoe through the brush, searching the shore for any point of elevation or potential campsite. Once, Aaron waded through knee-deep muck to look over a marked clearing on the south shore only to be chased back to the canoe by a thick cloud of bugs.

It was irritable work tunneling through this labyrinth. Branches scraped against our itchy bodies and showered us with dried leaves and spider webs as we continued in our confused attempts at maneuvering the sixteen-foot canoe through the constant twists and turns of the tortuous river.

Four hours later, just as abruptly as the alder thickets had closed in on us, the walls of brush thinned out and gave way to an open stand of spruce, balsam and a few white pines.

We made camp near the take-out of a 265-yard (240 m) portage marked on the left bank. We were both exhausted, and Aaron agreed to roll out the sleeping bags inside the tent while I cooked us a quick, hot meal. A

The beach site along Rosebary Lake's northeast shoreline is thought to be the location of one of the oldest Indian camps in the park.

few minutes later, while I had the noodles simmering on the cook stove, I pulled back the front tent flap to see how my partner was doing with the sleeping arrangements. I found him strewn out across both Therm-a-Rests, snoring away.

The next morning we headed down the river early to beat the bugs. We were rewarded with the sight of half a dozen moose at the entrance to Grass Lake — a shallow basin attached to the western fringe of the Nipissing River.

The route leaves the Nipissing shortly after the lake and heads south up Loontail Creek. It takes some doing to spot the narrow channel (look for where the two valleys split). The entrance to the creek is on the right bank, just before a point of land laden with cone-shaped spruce trees.

Loontail Creek meanders past fallen logs, around mudflats, and through shallow ponds bubbling with the stench of swamp gas. Eventually the creek becomes unnavigable. A 925-yard (845 m) portage, marked on the right bank, leads to another tributary, Latour Creek.

At the take-out, while I filtered the almost-stagnant creek water into our Nalgene bottles, Aaron sat down on a rotten tree stump for a smoke break. I teased him about his bad habit, whereupon he began to brag about how the smoke worked as a bug repellent. He then slipped his bug net back down over his face, with his cigarette still dangling from his lips. The butt instantly made a nickel-sized hole in the fine mesh. Moments later, the blackflies were making use of the new vestibule.

A logging road cuts across the portage midway up a moderate slope. I was disappointed at having to walk across yet another dusty roadway, especially when I had to stop to let a fully loaded diesel truck pass by. I released the pressure of the tumpline on my forehead to glance up at the driver, who was waving hello and toasting me with a can of cold Coke. On my second trip, for the canoe, I had grown infuriated with the intrusion. When I reached the road again, I heard another truck rattling down the roadway. This time I defiantly walked out to the middle, insistent that this driver stop for me.

I'm no radical anti-logger; in fact, I graduated as a forest technician a few years back. But to taunt a sweaty, bug-bitten portager with a frosted can of Coke was simply not acceptable! In any case, the second driver geared down and graciously let me cross, this time raising a can of Diet Sprite.

On the map, Latour Creek looks simple, cutting a fairly clear path through the land. But after the tedious obstacles we encountered on the other previous waterways, Aaron and I knew better. We were not surprised when the creek began to twist and turn more and more uncontrollably the farther we headed west of the put-in.

This time, however, we took advantage of our secluded surroundings and patiently paddled upstream, searching out brook trout in deep pools and under fallen trees torn away from the eroded banks. Before we reached the halfway point, where a weedy pond on the right links together with the creek, our stringer was full of brookies.

Eventually, the channel narrowed to just a little wider than the canoe. For a good forty minutes, Aaron and I followed a ritual of stepping in and out of our durable Royalex craft to drag it over shallow spots. By the time we reached the take-out for the portage that heads to Floating Heart Lake, the creek had disappeared under a litter of driftwood and alder branches.

The Floating Lake portage is the longest en route (1,500 yards [1,370 m]), and works its way over to the next watershed, alternating between steep climbs and muddy depressions. After the lake, only a level 400-yard (365 m) portage remains on the opposite shore before you reach Rosebary Lake.

There is a breathtaking stretch of beach along the northeast shoreline of Rosebary Lake. The beach site is thought to be the location of one of the oldest Indian camps in the park. Natives, while traveling between Georgian

Moose sighting number six along the upper Nipissing.

Bay and the Petawawa River, would stay on Rosebary Lake to collect the reddish clay from the lake's bottom for use as paint.

Aaron and I stopped off at the beach for a refreshing swim. It would have been great to stay at the adjoining campsite on the northern tip, but the spot was already occupied; so we paddled farther south to make camp near where Longbow Lake joins with Rosebary. (The lakes were coupled after the Booth Lumber Company constructed a dam on the Tim River.)

An evening breeze blew across our site, chasing away most of the bugs, and Aaron and I celebrated our last night in the park by baking a carrot cake and opening the remaining carton of white wine. My greenhorn partner was finally becoming comfortable with his surroundings — perhaps too comfortable.

Around midnight, a black bear wandered into our camp, probably smelling the remains of our cake smoldering in the fire. Aaron was still sound asleep as the bear — snorting and sniffing for more leftover baked goods — approached the tent.

Instinctively I slapped my hand against the nylon wall, yelling, "Go on! Get out!" I managed to scare the bruin off and at the same time startle the hell out of my brother-in-law. Later on, when the bear returned for another sniff around the camp, Aaron seemed content with me on watch and managed to sleep soundly through a second barrage of warning calls and tent bashing.

At the northeastern tip of Rosebary Lake, a weedy delta marks the entrance to the Tim River. The route continues here, leading upstream and back to Tim Lake. Apart from meandering through some dense patches of alder and overactive beaver dams, the channel is more direct than the Nipissing, making the trip back only a half-day's paddle.

Only one portage (130 yards [120 m]) is required, three-quarters of the way along. The steep path is well marked to the left of a falls. At the put-in, look for remnants of an elaborate lift built by the Booth Lumber Company. The loggers, who had a base camp on Tim Lake, hauled their square timber all the way from Longbow Lake and used the lift to drag it up the side of the cascade.

Make sure you stay to your right when paddling away from the falls. Navigating across the large swamp, cluttered with huge weathered tree trunks anchored in the silt, can be bewildering at times; in fact, when Aaron and I paddled across, we blindly mistook the narrow inlet to the left for the river and found ourselves lost for a spell in Shawshaw Lake, adding yet another mishap to my brother-in-law's first canoe expedition.

We endured the three-day ordeal — bugs and all. And after reminiscing about our wilderness experience, Aaron agreed that with a proper spring flood and a good supply of bug repellent, the Rosebary loop wouldn't have been half bad.

Rosebary Lake Loop

TIME
3 days

DIFFICULTY
Moderate to high

PORTAGES
15

LONGEST PORTAGE
1,500 yards (1,370 m)

Looking way up to the treetops in one of Algonquin's rare stands of 300-year-old pine, a highlight of the Crow Lake route.

Big Crow Lake

I HAVE TWO UNFORGETTABLE MEMORIES OF WORKING WITH the gang at the Boston Mills Press (my publishing company for the past ten years). The first is when the publisher, John Denison, and managing editor, Noel Hudson, arrived at my wedding dressed in beaver costumes and my four-year-old nephew — dubious of their authenticity — grabbed Noel by the crotch and then belted out, "You're not real!" The second is a canoe trip we shared to Algonquin's Big Crow Lake.

Accompanied by Michael Cullen, a photographer friend, I drove to the Lake Opeongo access point (4 miles [6 km] north of Highway 60), and met John and Noel, who were waiting inside the permit office.

To save us a day of paddling the rough waters of Lake Opeongo, we agreed to splurge and pay for a boat shuttle. Taxi service is offered by both Algonquin Outfitters and Opeongo Outfitters, and it takes just twenty minutes to transport you and your canoe to the Proulx Lake portage, on the northeast side of Opeongo's North Arm.

For our pickup time, the rules were simple. Our driver informed us that she would arrive at the Proulx Lake portage dock two days later, at *exactly* 1:30 p.m., and that, if no one was there to greet her, she would wait *exactly* fifteen minutes before heading back. We all smirked at our driver's dogmatic approach; after all, we had already paid for the return trip. We all but ignored her firm protocol and waved goodbye.

The Proulx Lake portage is an easy walk, but not far from the take-out, where the trail splits, the route is a bit confusing. The main path (1,520 yards [1,390 m]) is to the right, skirting a shallow pond by going up and over an eroded hummock littered with exposed tree roots. The flatter path, to the left, is a cart trail (used for carrying boats and gear on two-wheel dollies), and heads to a pond, which must be paddled before you join up with the main portage. The choice is yours. Mike and Noel chose to paddle across the pond and save themselves a good chunk of the portage. John and I opted for the more direct route to the right and ended up at the finish well before the others.

The route continues across Proulx Lake and eventually heads left down the third and largest bay, marked by a campsite situated high atop a sandy point and surrounded by a prominent stand of red pine.

A weedy creek connects Proulx with Little Crow Lake, and took us a little more than an hour to paddle (a cow moose wading in midstream slowed our progress somewhat). Once at Little Crow we kept to the right and entered Big Crow Lake by way of a wide channel (look for a small island marking the entranceway).

There is not a single ugly campsite on Big Crow. Our preference, however, was one of a cluster of beach sites just to the left of the Crow River. We camped both nights on the same site so that we could spend the entire second day exploring the lake.

First we checked out the stand of virgin white pine to the east. The three-hundred-year-old trees were legally protected from logging in 1939 by the noteworthy park superintendent Frank MacDougall. Saving this majestic stand was part of MacDougall's plan to establish a standard system of shoreline timber reserves for the entire park. In 1976, in honor of MacDougall's foresight into the ever-increasing conflict between logging and recreational use in Algonquin, the park section of Highway 60 was renamed the Frank MacDougall Parkway.

The original trail leading to the stand of pine began near the put-in of the first portage along the Crow River. The twenty-minute walk headed off to the right, cut across the waterway over the remains of the washed-out logging dam, climbed up an abrupt embankment, and then worked itself inland. But a new put-in has recently been established at the far end of the bay, to the right of the portage, avoiding the river altogether.

After leaving the majestic stand of pine, our Crow Lake tour continued to the ranger's cabin situated along the western shore of the lake's southern bay. The cabin, built initially for the ranger who manned the Crow Lake fire tower (constructed in 1956), was one of the last ranger cabins to be erected in the park.

In 1931, to fight fires throughout the park's interior, Frank MacDougall organized a network of steel towers, telephone lines and fire crews. He also acquired a bush plane, which he piloted himself. Eventually though, radios made the high-maintenance telephone wires strung throughout the bush obsolete. The fire towers were abandoned in 1975, leaving fire detection solely to patrolling aircraft.

The trail to the Crow Lake fire tower begins behind and to the left of the cabin, and it takes a good twenty minutes to clamber up to the site. For safety reasons, the park staff have removed the last rung of steps at the base of the tower. But Mike and Noel were not going to let a few missing steps stop them from climbing up. They made it to the top, but after being taunted by graffiti — "Don't fall now" and "The last step's a doozy" — on the way up, and tip-toeing on the spongy floor-boards of the wooden cabin

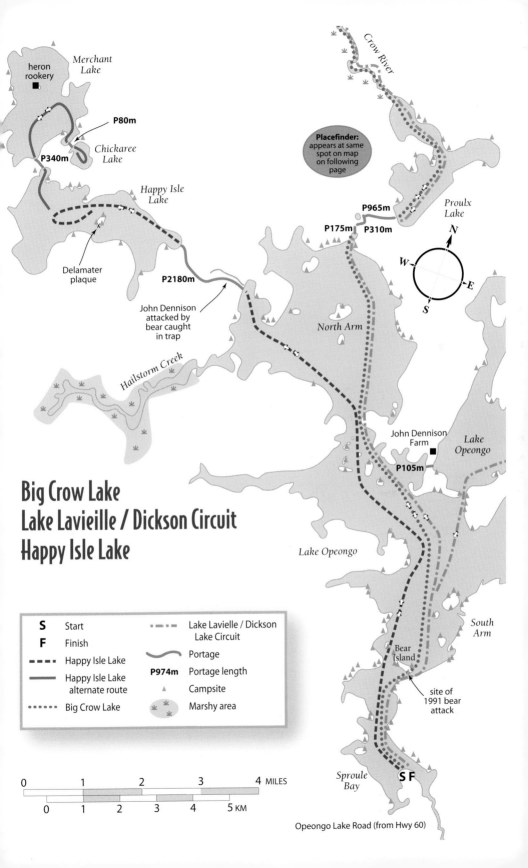

Merchant Lake

heron rookery ■

P80m

P340m

Chickaree Lake

Crow River

Placefinder: appears at same spot on map on following page

Proulx Lake

Happy Isle Lake

P965m

P175m   **P310m**

X

Delamater plaque

N

W   **E**

S

P2180m

John Dennison attacked by bear caught in trap

North Arm

Hailstorm Creek

John Dennison Farm ■

Lake Opeongo

P105m

Big Crow Lake
Lake Lavieille / Dickson Circuit
Happy Isle Lake

Lake Opeongo

South Arm

Bear Island

site of 1991 bear attack

S	Start
F	Finish
– – –	Happy Isle Lake
——	Happy Isle Lake alternate route
·····	Big Crow Lake
–·–·–	Lake Lavielle / Dickson Lake Circuit
∿	Portage
P974m	Portage length
▲	Campsite
✿	Marshy area

S F

Sproule Bay

0   1   2   3   4 MILES

0   1   2   3   4   5 KM

Opeongo Lake Road (from Hwy 60)

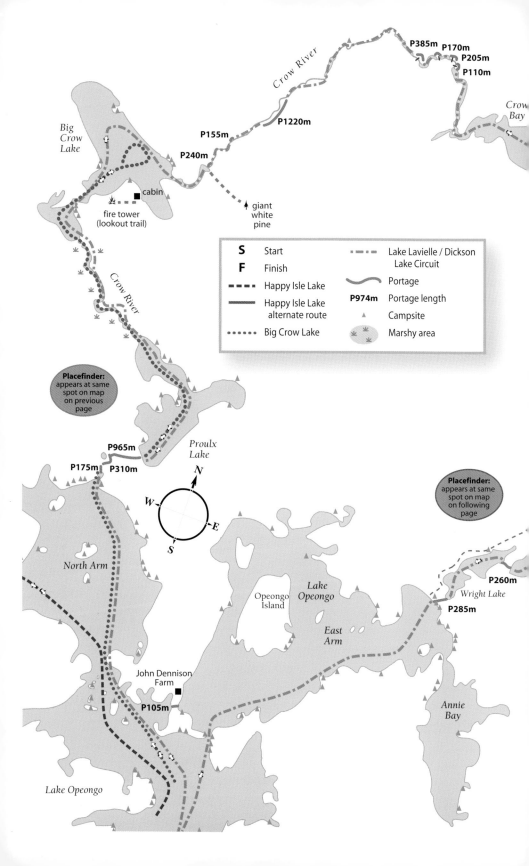

Crow River

P385m
P170m
P205m
P110m

Crow Bay

Big Crow Lake

P1220m

P155m

P240m

cabin

fire tower (lookout trail)

giant white pine

Crow River

| S | Start |
| F | Finish |

Happy Isle Lake
Happy Isle Lake alternate route
Big Crow Lake

Lake Lavielle / Dickson Lake Circuit
Portage
P974m Portage length
▲ Campsite
Marshy area

Placefinder: appears at same spot on map on previous page

Placefinder: appears at same spot on map on following page

P965m

P175m P310m

Proulx Lake

N
W — E
S

North Arm

Opeongo Island

Lake Opeongo

East Arm

Wright Lake

P260m

P285m

John Dennison Farm

P105m

Annie Bay

Lake Opeongo

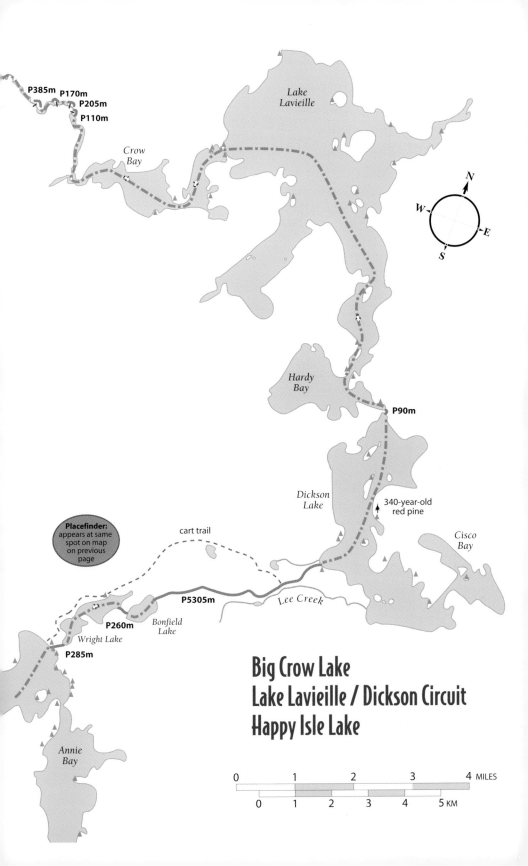

P385m P170m
        P205m
        P110m

*Lake
Lavieille*

*Crow
Bay*

N
W   E
S

*Hardy
Bay*

P90m

*Dickson
Lake*

340-year-old
red pine

*Cisco
Bay*

Placefinder:
appears at same
spot on map
on previous
page

cart trail

Lee Creek

P5305m

P260m *Bonfield
Lake*

Wright Lake

P285m

Big Crow Lake
Lake Lavieille / Dickson Circuit
Happy Isle Lake

*Annie
Bay*

0   1   2   3   4 MILES

0   1   2   3   4   5 KM

All campsites on Crow Lake are great, but the all-time favorite is the beach site alongside the mouth of the Crow River.

that rests precariously at the top, they both agreed that continuing past the tower to the lookout on the ground level is a much more comfortable way to view the scenic landscape. Take note that in 2011 during a lightning storm the top of the tower "flew" off.

It was late in the day when we ended our sightseeing, and Noel and Mike, still on a high from their daredevil maneuvers up on the tower, rushed ahead of John and me to get a fire started for dinner. Their enthusiasm was soon dampened, however, when I walked up the beach with a pot of water and doused their campfire, reminding them of the total fire ban that had been placed on the park interior.

For a good hour, Mike and Noel bickered with me, arguing that it was a sin to fry up choice tenderloin on the flames of a mere camp stove, especially after an afternoon rain shower had moistened the forest floor enough to remove any fire ban (we later learned that the ban had been lifted that very afternoon). But rules are rules; besides, it was my name on the camp permit.

The next morning we enjoyed a breakfast of bacon and eggs — fried on the camp stove, of course — and then left Big Crow Lake the same way we arrived. With our lazy paddle strokes, countless stops for snacks and juice, and an extended photo session with the same moose we encountered on the way in, we were five minutes late arriving at the Proulx Lake portage. We weren't really concerned about our tardiness, that is, not until another group of canoeists traveling the portage in the opposite direction informed us that our ride was leaving. I instantly unbuckled my pack, tossed it aside, and sprinted to the end of the portage.

The boat had already left the dock when I arrived (it was 1:47 p.m.). Luckily for us, the engine had stalled while the shuttle driver was drifting the boat over a nearby shoal. I shouted and signaled her back while the rest of the crew hurried along with our baggage. We were glad not to have missed the boat; the wind had built up swells, and it would have been impossible to paddle back. After a stern "I told you so" from the driver, we made our apologies and enjoyed a quick, safe passage across Lake Opeongo.

Big Crow Lake

TIME
2 to 3 days
(4 days without taking the water taxi)

DIFFICULTY
Novice

PORTAGES
2

LONGEST PORTAGE
1,585 yards
(1,450 m)

Lake Lavieille has to be one of the most picturesque lakes in the park.

Lake Lavieille/Dickson Circuit

IT'S NOT THAT I DISLIKE THE OTHER CANOEISTS that gather on some of the more popular routes in Algonquin; they're all trying to escape the same city sirens and traffic jams that I am. But after having to deal with an angry mob assembled out on busy Canoe Lake, Alana and I finally decided to avoid the masses and headed out on the more remote Lake Lavieille/ Dickson circuit instead. The seclusion of this route comes at a high price — a grueling portage measuring over 3 miles (5 km) in length!

The access point is Lake Opeongo, located 4 miles (6.2 km) north, off Highway 60. From the docks, the route heads straight up Opeongo to the North Arm's Proulx Lake portage. The trip across Opeongo takes a full day, that is, if the winds don't play havoc with your canoe and leave you stranded halfway. To give ourselves extra time to explore the more remote Lavieille and Dickson Lakes, Alana and I chose to pay for a boat shuttle to the Proulx Lake portage (reservations for the water taxi can be made with either Algonquin Outfitters or Opeongo Outfitters), and by mid-afternoon we found ourselves camped on Big Crow Lake's beach site, by the mouth of the Crow River (see Big Crow Lake for a route description).

Early the next morning, fueled by a stack of flapjacks and camp coffee, we were on our way east, down the Crow River. A ten-minute paddle brought us to the first portage, measuring 265 yards (240 m) and marked to the left. The trail works its way around the debris of an old logging dam and then cuts through what remains of one of the largest logging camps in Algonquin, owned and operated by the McLaughlin Brothers.

After the first portage, the river continues to drop over a series of shallow rock gardens (which makes upstream travel difficult for those who choose to follow the route counterclockwise). It then eases up just before the take-out for the second portage, which measures 170 yards (155 m) and is also marked to the left. Except for the odd riffle, the current is slow and meandering before you reach the third and largest portage along the river. The take-out is to the right this time, with the 1,335-yard (1,220 m) trail leading through a patch of second-growth pine and crossing a well-used logging road three-quarters of the way along.

After the portage, you're in for an hour-and-a-half paddle through a slow, meandering stretch of river. Here, the banks are lined with groves of tamarack and an unbelievable display of purple iris. At each oxbow, deep pools harbor native brook trout, and marsh flats are rife with moose (Alana and

I counted seven in total). The river's only campsite is also found halfway along this section of Crow River. The site is marked to the left, high up on a sandy embankment and in among a rare stand of jack pine. This fire-dependent species started to disappear from the park after a controversial fire-suppression policy was put in place during the writing of Algonquin's Timber Management Plan.

The quickwater soon continues, and four rapids run in succession just before the river filters out into Lake Lavieille's Crow Bay. The first swift is avoided by way of a 420-yard (385 m) portage to the left (watch your step at the rocky put-in). The three remaining, each with their own portage (185, 225 and 120 yards [170, 205 and 110 m], all marked to the left) could be lined or waded down in summer, and are possibly runnable earlier in the season.

Approximately one-and-a-half miles (2 km) from the last drop, where a small tributary flows in from the west, the river takes a dramatic twist to the left and enters Big Crow Bay. If you stay to the center of the bay while making your way across from the marshy outlet, keeping an eye out for two orange campsite markers on the left and right of a small island, you should easily find the inlet joining Big Crow Bay with Lake Lavieille. The narrows makes a quick turn to the north shortly after you enter from the bay and then heads east again before a cluster of choice campsites at the entrance to the lake.

When Alana and I arrived at Lake Lavieille, the winds were picking up and black-bottomed clouds were beginning to speed by overhead. Not wanting to find ourselves weather-bound the next day on the lake's more exposed northern end, we took advantage of the calm before the storm. We were able to reach an island campsite, protected by the north shore of a gigantic inlet to the southwest, before the rain pelted down.

With our rain tarp stretched over the reasonably dry fire ring, we were able to make the best of it during the storm. In fact, our outdoor kitchen became quite cozy, and after dinner we spiced our nightly tea with Bailey's Irish Cream, huddled close together in front of the smoldering fire, and took great pleasure in being totally alone.

Lavieille has always been one of the most secluded lakes in the park. This seclusion was further ensured on December 22, 1993, when the MNR announced that Lake Lavieille, along with Dickson Lake to the south, was to be part of the park's new wilderness zone. The area — measuring 62,500 acres (25,000 hectares) — is estimated to contain 40 percent of the remaining red and white pine old-growth forest in Algonquin. It is now off limits to logging, automobiles and motorboats.

The next morning, the high winds were still howling across the expanse of Lake Lavieille. But by hugging the shoreline, Alana and I were able to make our way slowly down the southern inlet to Hardy Bay. From there, we stayed to our left and crossed over the quick, 100-yard (90 m) portage to Dickson Lake.

Dickson Lake is named after James Dickson, who, with his colleague Alexander Kirkwood, was the first to lobby for the development of Algonquin Park in 1893. Both brook and lake trout thrive in Dickson's deep, almost turquoise waters, and the clumps of 340-year-old red pine that stretch out from the more dominant white pine growing along the eastern shoreline are impressive. But, because of its popularity, Alana and I found the campsites far less desirable. The first two sites we inspected, along the west shore, were particularly disappointing. Anglers had left a homemade live well — made of chicken wire and metal stakes — anchored along the shoreline, and a bear had recently rummaged through both sites, overturning logs placed around the campfire and digging up one of the latrines to get at a discarded can of Spam.

We ended up choosing a campsite on a nearby island. The spot was well used, judging by the initials carved into a few birch trees and a collection of camp grills left behind to rust in the back bush. But it was, nonetheless, a beautiful site, with a clear view of almost the entire lake. Still reveling in the fact that we had not spotted a single canoeist since Big Crow Lake, we sat out on the spit until the sun set and the mosquitoes began to swarm out from the backwoods for their nightly feeding frenzy.

We awoke early the next day, eager to meet the challenge awaiting us at the far end of the western bay: the infamous Dickson/Bonfield portage! Days before, agreeing that a double carry would be suicidal, we had decided to pack only the bare essentials so as to enable us to carry over the extensive 5,800-yard (5,305 m) trail in one trip. We estimated that by stopping for a five-minute rest every twenty minutes, we would find ourselves at the put-in in approximately two hours (the record is forty-one minutes, set by Bill Swift Sr. while carrying a canvas-covered canoe and a loaded pack).

With Alana carrying a gigantic pack, and I loaded down with a smaller pack and the canoe (thank goodness for Kevlar), we headed out along the relatively flat trail at exactly 9:45 a.m.

Our first break ended at a fork in the portage. The right branch is marked as a cart trail, and the left branch is the regular portage to Bonfield Lake.

Three breaks later — at 11:22 a.m. — we arrived at the other end, amazed at having completed the ordeal in only an hour and thirty-seven minutes,

Alana and I celebrate after completing the dreaded Dickson/Bonfield portage in a mere one hour and thirty-seven minutes.

(once you have reached a logging road you know you are past the halfway point). Of course, the sight of fresh bear prints and steaming piles of dung all along the trail may have speeded our progress. In any case, Alana and I celebrated our achievement by lighting up a couple of cigars. (We're both non-smokers, but we figured that after an ordeal like that it was okay to break a few rules.)

Two short portages (285 and 315 yards [260 and 285 m]) and a quick paddle across Lakes Bonfield and Wright were all that remained before we arrived at Lake Opeongo's east arm. Upon arriving at the big lake, most canoe-ists take a prescheduled water taxi back to the parking lot. But Alana and I, deciding to save the expense of a second shuttle, planned on making our way back by canoe.

We had originally intended to spend our last night camped somewhere along the East Arm. But when we arrived at Opeongo, the waters were unusually calm — something we've learned to take full advantage of during previous trips on Algonquin's largest lake. We canceled any ideas of an early camp and began making our way down the East Arm.

Two hours from the put-in we stopped for a late lunch at the site of the Dennison Farm. The clearing of the Sunnyside settlement is to the right of the narrows leading into the main body of the lake and is marked by Captain John Dennison's gravesite (a fenced-in plot with a copper plaque reading "At Rest").

The death of the eighty-two-year-old pioneer, who was once a captain in the military, was a tragic one. Dennison and his eight-year-old grandson were out checking a bear trap set a week earlier along the Happy Isle portage. When the captain walked up to the trap, he was surprised by the wounded occupant of the steel-clawed leghold.

Amazingly, Dennison's grandson paddled the 9 miles (15 km) back to the homestead for help. By the time the boy returned with his father, however, both Captain John and the bear were found dead.

Alana and I hurried our stay at the Dennison site, thinking we still had enough daylight to make it all the way back to the access point. But once we had paddled through the southern narrows and were halfway across the width of Jones Bay, the wind picked up, and dark, anvil-shaped clouds drifted in from the west.

With the swells out on the lake quickly growing to an unmanageable size, Alana and I knew that making it back to the parking lot was just wishful thinking; so, seeking shelter from the coming storm, we allowed the canoe to lurch indecisively through the chop until we reached the lee side of a cluster of islands. It wasn't my favorite place to make camp. Not that the site wasn't protected from the high winds barreling down the expanse of Opeongo. It wasn't that at all. The problem was, in my bear-phobic opinion, that we were marooned a little too close to Bates Island — the same island where, on October 11, 1991, Raymond Jakubauskas and Carola Frehe were killed by a bear.

Lake Lavieille / Dickson Circuit

TIME
4 to 6 days

DIFFICULTY
Moderate level of experience is needed, but bring light-weight gear and a Kevlar canoe if you want to survive the Dickson / Bonfield portage.

PORTAGES
12

LONGEST PORTAGE
5,800 yards (5,305 m), the longest in the park

The two campers met a horrible fate. The bear, apparently a healthy eight-year-old male weighing 310 pounds (140 kg), first attacked Carola and then turned on Raymond after he attempted to drive the bear off with an oar. It is believed that they both died quickly from single blows to the head. For five full days, however, the bear dragged the bodies back away from the site, feeding off them, and then covering them with leaves. When the park staff recovered the bodies (and shot the bear), they were 140 yards (125 m) from the campsite.

Reports state that the campers, soon after arriving on the island, were in the midst of preparing dinner when they were attacked, but all of the food, including an exposed tray of ground beef, was left untouched when park staff arrived a full week later. This was no nuisance "garbage" bear; it was a predaceous killer.

Of course, statistics show that you have a much greater chance of being killed in a car accident while driving along the Highway 60 corridor than you do of being attacked by a predaceous bear. Before the 1991 incident, the last account of an Algonquin bear killing its victims as prey was in 1978.

But statistical analysis didn't ease my fears through the stormy night, and I stayed awake in the fetal position, jumping at every shadow that bounced off the tent wall. By morning I was exhausted. I lay there beside my wife, who had slept soundly through my hours of vulnerability.

Early that morning, Alana and I headed south, back to the parking lot, to end our trip and begin the long, dangerous drive along the Highway 60 corridor.

Three Mile Lake Loop

MOST FIRST-TIME VISITORS TO ALGONQUIN'S NORTH END STAY on either North Tea Lake or Manitou Lake. There's no question that both lakes offer prime campsites and incredible scenery, but once you have experienced a weekend of listening to the constant drone of gas-leaking outboards breaking the morning silence (motors of 10 horsepower or less are permitted on both North Tea and Manitou), you'll soon realize why many park regulars choose to escape the hustle and bustle of the main lakes and head farther in to the more isolated interior.

One of the best four-day routes in the area is a loop connecting North Tea, Biggar, Three Mile and Manitou Lakes. The put-in is at Kawawaymog Lake. To reach the access point from Highway 11, turn east onto Ottawa Avenue in South River. The access is approximately 14 miles (22 km) from South River to the park gatehouse and government docks.

The first day has you paddling east from the access point toward Biggar Lake (see Nipissing Loop for a route description). The route then continues from the northeast end of Biggar Lake to Three Mile Lake. These two larger lakes are connected by Sinclair, Kawa and Upper Kawa Lakes, and by four very steep portages (520, 1,050, 350 and 1,230 yards [475, 960, 320 and 1,125 m]). This is the roughest section of the trip and I strongly suggest that you plan on going no farther than the campsites located in Three Mile Lake's southern bay on your second day out.

An alternative route takes advantage of the swollen creeks to the southeast of Biggar Lake during early spring and extends the loop for an extra two or three days. It was a year ago that my regular fishing buddies and I tried out this more adventurous route; we found it to be an incredibly grueling ordeal. But with any hardship comes reward, and apart from the trials of traveling through this low-maintenance area of the park, each member of our party came back with a real sense of accomplishment.

The endurance test began the moment we got to Birchcliffe Creek. It took four hours of tunneling through thick patches of alder, lifting over countless logjams, and racing the canoe up miniature swifts, before we reached the first portage. And typical of any of the less-traveled routes in Algonquin, the take-out to the 285-yard (260 m) trail was unmarked. The only clue we had that a portage even existed was that the narrow, twisting waterway suddenly became unnavigable. We eventually had to backtrack to find the trail.

A ten-minute paddle from the previous portage brought us to where the

Three Mile Lake Loop

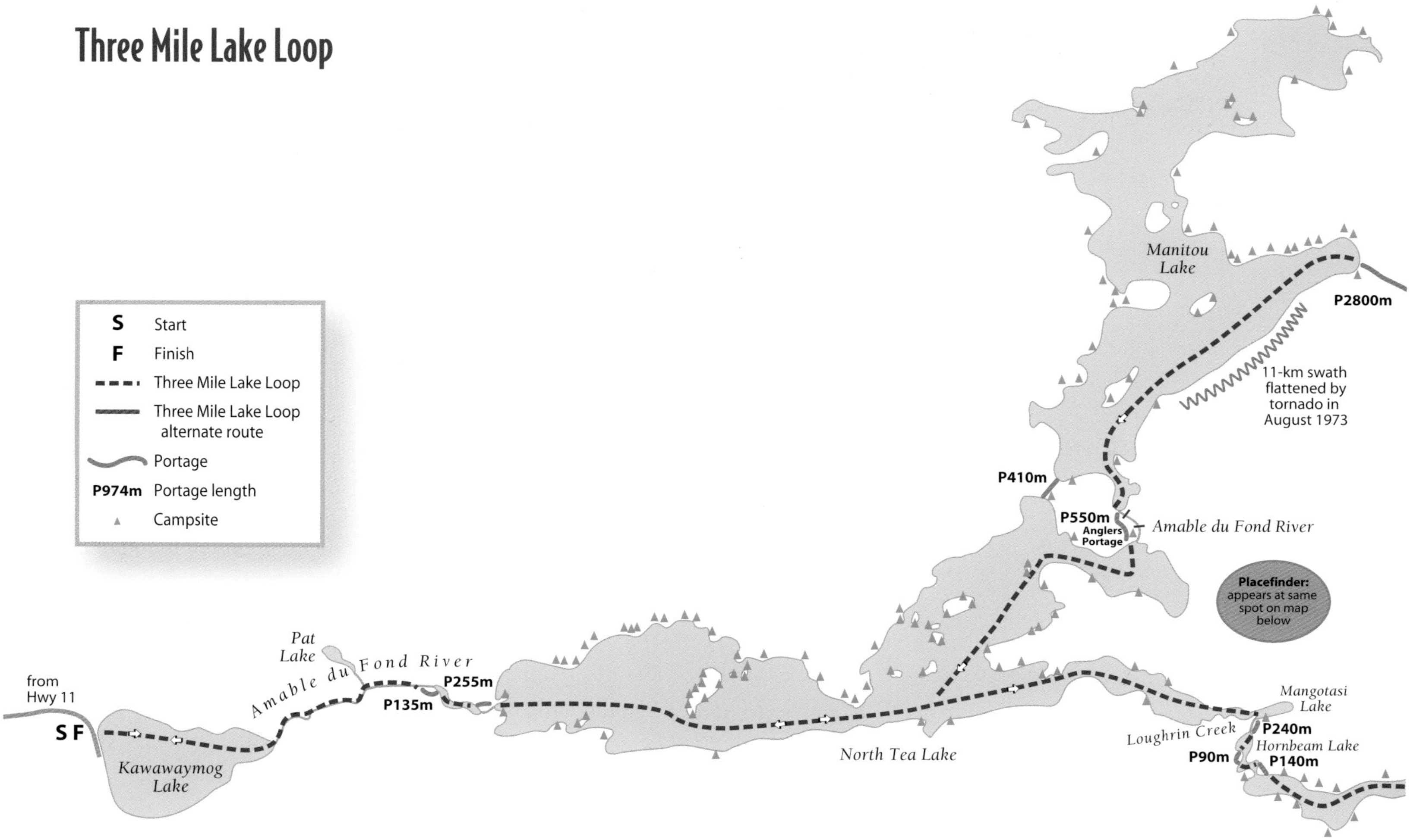

Legend:

S	Start
F	Finish
- - -	Three Mile Lake Loop
——	Three Mile Lake Loop alternate route
⌒	Portage
P974m	Portage length
▲	Campsite

P2800m

11-km swath flattened by tornado in August 1973

Amable du Fond River

Placefinder: appears at same spot on map below

Manitou Lake

P550m

Anglers Portage

P410m

Mangotasi Lake

Loughrin Creek

P240m

Hornbeam Lake

P140m

P90m

North Tea Lake

Amable du Fond River

P255m

P135m

Pat Lake

Kawawaymog Lake

from Hwy 11

S F

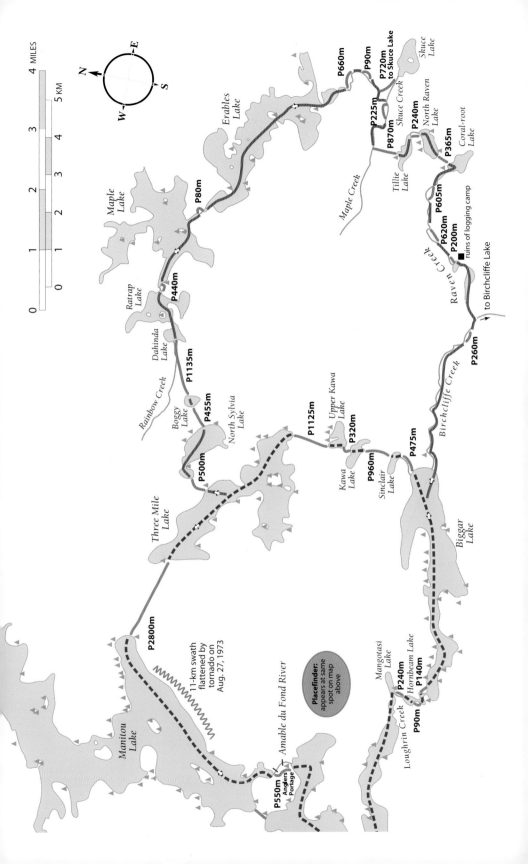

N

W — E — S

0 1 2 3 4 MILES

5 KM
0 1 2 3 4 5

Maple Lake

Erables Lake

P660m

P90m

P720m to Skuce Lake

Skuce Lake

P225m

P870m

Skuce Creek

P240m

North Raven Lake

P365m

Coral-root Lake

P605m

P620m

P200m

ruins of logging camp

Raven Creek

to Birchcliffe Lake

Tillie Lake

Maple Creek

P80m

Ratrap Lake

P440m

Dahinda Lake

Rainbow Creek

P1135m

Boggy Lake

P455m

North Sylvia Lake

P500m

Three Mile Lake

P2800m

11-km swath flattened by tornado on Aug. 27, 1973

Manitou Lake

Amable du Fond River

P550m Anders Portage

P1125m

Upper Kawa Lake

P320m

Kawa Lake

P960m

Sinclair Lake

P475m

Birchcliffe Creek

P260m

Biggar Lake

Placefinder: appears at same spot on map above

Mangotasi Lake

P240m

Hornbeam Lake

P140m

P90m

Loughrin Creek

Being windbound can be frustrating at times (Manitou Lake).

waterway splits. We kept to the left, away from Birchcliffe, and headed up an even narrower channel called Raven Creek. By the end of June, this route would be impossible; even if water levels were still high, the insects would eat you alive. But it was only the second week in May, and conditions were perfect for us; the creeks were in flood and the blackflies had yet to hatch. In fact, mounds of snow still remained in the bush — giving rise to several snowball fights — and chunks of ice clung to the edges of the two connecting ponds a short paddle upstream on Raven Creek.

At the far end of the second pond, at an old logging camp, we stopped for lunch. The site was a treasure trove of artifacts, from crosscut saws and piles of discarded horseshoes, to crumbled shanties with iron bunks and potbelly stoves. Even two water-tank sleighs, scarred with numerous vertical bear-claw marks, stood in the back field (the sleighs would have been filled with icy lake water and hauled down the winter roads during the night to leave an icy surface for moving logs the next day). But the most impressive thing about this find was that it was left mostly unmolested — something that has become a rarity in Algonquin Park.

After spending time exploring the ruins, we made a quick paddle east of the logging camp to begin the second portage of the day: a 220-yard (200 m) trail cluttered with an entanglement of blow downs. It was an easy carry, though, compared to the next two portages (688 and 660 yards [620 and 605 m]), marked on the right bank of Raven Creek.

The trail was littered with deadfall, and mud-filled gullies were frequent. At first we tried going around the debris, but detouring through the thick brush would only have been possible if our elongated tripping canoes were equipped with articulated steering. Instead, we were forced to slide the canoes over the trunks of the downed trees and then slug our gear underneath like a group of overdressed limbo dancers.

At one point, while carrying across the second of the two portages, we lost our way completely. The trail, after heading through a stand of maples, made use of an overgrown logging road. Near the top of a moderate slope, however, the portage made a sudden turn to the left, back into the obscurity of dense vegetation. A dull, colored ribbon tied to yet another fallen tree was the only indication that the portage left the road. Five of us had already passed the turn-off point and continued down the road before Peter, who had luckily stopped for a swig of juice, noticed the marker and called us all back.

Three hours later, with our canoes scratched and gouged by branches, we reached the deep waters of Coral-root Lake. Before rounding the bend to the north and beginning another portage — a steep, 400-yard (365 m) trail leading to North Raven Lake — we took a break and filtered fresh water into our Nalgene bottles. While I mixed Tang crystals with the cool water, my partner, Scott, made sandwiches with bannock, sliced cheese, and a fresh tomato that had miraculously escaped being squished in the food pack.

Thinking back, we should have just stopped and made camp on Coral-root Lake or even North Raven Lake; both lakes were a shimmering turquoise, and each campsite was out on a rock outcrop and came with a shady patch of white pine. But Scott, who enjoys testing the limits of his own — and everyone else's — endurance, coached the group into continuing on. We paddled to the top end of North Raven Lake, portaged the 260 yards (240 m) into the less-than-scenic Tillie Lake, and were about to begin the 950-yard (870 m) portage to Maple Creek when a mutiny was staged.

We made camp directly beside the take-out to the 950-yard (870 m) portage. It was a disappointing spot — just enough space to crowd our three tents together on a cleared patch in a patchwork of scraggly spruce — but we made the best of it. In the fading light of a golden evening, we sat around a smoldering fire, sipping on gin and cherry Kool-Aid from our enamel cups while Scott prepared dinner.

Early the next morning we had a quick breakfast of oatmeal and coffee and then hauled our gear directly from the campsite to Maple Creek. At the other end of the creek was yet another narrow, twisting channel choked with alders. This time, however, it was a downstream run. We were so used to the long, convoluted struggle upstream that the quick ride made it seem as though we'd gotten off easy.

Soon the waterway was blocked again, not by downed cedars, but by a newly constructed logging road. With this open wound, the area's wilderness appeal quickly vanished. The only good that came of it was that the 245-yard (225 m) portage, marked a short distance after, was a well-worn trail, free of any blow downs.

A ten-minute paddle from the put-in of the maintained portage, where Maple Creek curves northward (the Skuce Lake portage is marked to the right), the waterway finally begins to widen its banks. At this point, two portages (both marked on the right) remain on Maple Creek: a quick, 100 yards (90 m) around a small falls, and a longer, 720 yards (660 m) leading to what remains of Maple Creek before it flushes into the south end of Erables Lake.

Lakes Erables and Maple, connected by a 90-yard (80 m) portage to the right of another scenic cascade, were a welcome paddle. Finally out in the open, we took advantage of a tail wind and leaned back to watch the birdlife along the shore; groupings of squabbling bluejays flapped among the pinhead spruce, a pair of siskins chased one another around a sunny branch of a red pine, and, from a grove of poplars, a single wood thrush, with its flute-like song, tried to compete with the piercing call of a white-throated sparrow.

By mid-afternoon, we found ourselves sailing into Maple Lake's north-western inlet to begin another series of portages. The first, leading into Ratrap Lake (one of the nicest lakes en route), is an easy 480 yards (440 m).

Next is a 1,240-yard (1,135 m) portage beginning at the western inlet of Ratrap and ending in oval-shaped Boggy Lake. The trail leads to the left, crosses a logging road a quarter of the way along, and then soon heads back into the bush.

The two remaining portages — 500 yards (455 m), from the west shore of Boggy Lake to North Sylvia, and 545 yards (500 m), from the northwest-ern inlet of North Sylvia Lake to Three Mile Lake — each take you over a hummock, but they are still relatively easy carries.

Three Mile Lake, where our group made camp on our third night out, marks the return to the regular route. The next morning we lingered over a second cup of coffee; so far, we had been on the water before 7 a.m. every morning, and we decided we were due for a lazy start. The winds began, strong and cold, on our way to the northwest end of Three Mile Lake, and by the time we began to unload the canoes at the start of the portage into Manitou Lake, a stiff breeze was blowing across the lake.

We were glad to find that the long, 3,060-yard (2,800 m) portage was fairly easy; a flat road made up for more than half its length, and the only difficult portion was the last quarter, where a downward slope gave our quadriceps a good workout.

Five minutes out from the put-in, the winds increased twofold, and the gusts quickly formed a barrage of waves. We scuttled plans to paddle south-west down the middle of Manitou to the main portage to North Tea Lake. Instead, we opted to stay close to the left-hand shoreline until we reached the lesser-known portage tucked away at the end of the southern inlet.

The gale, sifting through the second growth of birch and poplar rooted on shore, brought on more swells, and the lake soon demanded our full attention; after all, we were hugging the same shoreline where a tornado touched down in 1973, leveling a 7-mile (11 km) strip of forest.

Scott and I instinctively knelt, lowering the canoe's center of gravity and adding to its stability. At first we were able to keep a straight course;

Scott checks out the historic plaque commemorating park rangers F. X. Robichaud and Tom Wattie (North Tea Lake Lodge).

a routine of broad, sweeping strokes kept the canoe from the sideswiping waves. Soon, however, the smooth, rounded tops of the troughs began to break, and water splashed over the bow. Enough was enough, and the entire group quickly headed for shore.

Everyone was in a rotten mood. We had pushed ourselves hard for three days, and now, during the day that was supposed to be our shortest en route, the wind was holding us back. We tried to wait it out on a rocky point, taking the opportunity to recuperate. But, wind-bound on Manitou and still having the entire length of North Tea to contend with the next day, we began to fidget.

So, when the waves seemed to diminish a bit, I lobbied for departure and we made a beeline for the protective inlet to the south. The calm spell didn't last long, but we managed to make it safely into the bay, where the waves lost their angry white-capped chop.

We then scurried up the steep 600-yard (550 m) portage to the right of a magnificent cascade that tumbles down from North Tea Lake. At the put-in, where the gushing water seemed much more active than at the base of the falls, we made one more push against the turbulent wind. We finally made camp at 7:45 p.m.

We skipped the gin and Kool-Aid that night, and immediately went into frying up a lake trout I had caught out on Manitou (despite the wind, I had still trolled a line as we went). Content, we all tottered off to bed thinking our hardships were over — that is, until the storm hit!

At midnight I was awakened by approaching thunder. I tried to ignore it at first; the rumbling seemed a good distance away. But a sudden loud clap followed by a flash of lightning that lit up the inside of the tent jolted me into action. I rushed outside to check that the tent pegs were secure, the canoes tied down, and the packs piled under the tarp.

The rain changed from large, sporadic drops into a steady torrent in seconds. Then, just as I scurried back into the tent to escape the serious downpour, hurricane winds brought a volley of hailstones the size of golf balls.

The storm ended as quickly as it had arrived, and we all exited our tents to inspect the damage. A medium-sized tree had crashed down onto the outhouse, and poles from two of the three tents were bent beyond repair. Somehow, though, our tarp managed to stay up, and the canoe tie-downs held the boats firm on the beach.

Still shaken from the night's events, we found ourselves paddling at half-past six the next morning. The wind had died by now, and the lake was wrapped in a chilling mist. We took advantage of the calm to escape the expanse of North Tea Lake. In a few hours we were safe and sound at a roadside cafe, enjoying greasy food and pondering the past few days.

Why had we chosen the less-traveled route? Why had we pushed ourselves against the winds out on Manitou? Overconfidence, perhaps? A desire to test our skills and endurance and to ride the aftershock of adrenaline? Maybe. I do know that by the time we had finished our burgers and fries, we had already planned next year's trip — a longer, more rugged alternative route into the interior of Algonquin Park!

Three Mile Lake Loop

TIME
3 to 5 days

DIFFICULTY
Moderate tripping experience is needed if you choose to explore Birchcliffe and Raven Creek, and high winds can make travel on North Tea and Manitou Lakes extremely difficult.

PORTAGES
24

LONGEST PORTAGE
3,060 yards (2,800 m) mostly on a road

Solo tripping is definitely good for the soul.

Happy Isle Lake

IN 1988 MY FATHER DISCOVERED HE HAD LUNG cancer and his life suddenly, drastically changed; so did mine. After work, instead of driving home with my colleagues, I'd grab a quick dinner at a fast-food restaurant along the highway and then head for the hospital in time for visiting hours. For months this nightly routine went on, and so did my father's treatments. Eventually the cancer was successfully removed. When my father's physical healing process was finally over, I figured it was time for my mental healing to begin, and what better way than a solo canoe trip to Algonquin's Happy Isle Lake.

The route begins at Opeongo Lake, located 4 miles (6.2 km) north of Highway 60. My options were to either head up to the North Arm by taking the 20-minute boat shuttle (reservations can be made with either Algonquin Outfitters or Opeongo Outfitters) or paddle a full day to reach the portage leading into Happy Isle Lake. With Opeongo as smooth as a pond, I chose the paddling option, and by late afternoon I was camped on the site almost directly across from the Happy Isle take-out.

Early the next morning, after a quick paddle across to Hailstorm Creek for a look at the regular congregation of moose that browses near the mouth (I counted six in total), I began to the haul my gear across the 2,385-yard (2,180 m) portage to Happy Isle. It was a long hike, taking me just over an hour and a half to complete a double carry, but the trail was relatively flat, and, where it wasn't, I was able to rest my weighted canoe across a well-positioned canoe rest.

By mid-afternoon, I had made my way across to Happy Isle's only island and made camp on the second of three designated sites. Here, on a rock ledge, a decorative plaque overlooking the water marks the final camp of a father and son who drowned on this lake during a severe windstorm in 1931. It reads:

IN MEMORIAM
VAN NESS DELAMATER
AGED 53 YEARS.
VAN NESS DELAMATER JR.
AGED 23 YEARS.
LOST IN HURRICANE AUGUST 29 1931.
ALL IN THE CONFIDENCE AND PRIME OF MANHOOD,
ALL IN THE GLORY OF YOUTH'S ASPIRATION,
ONE WILD AND AWEFUL MOMENT, AND THEN — GOD.

A memorial plaque marks the favorite campsite of two canoeists who drowned on Happy Isle Lake, 1931.

When all hope of finding the drowned victims was gone, Mrs. A. Delamater asked that the plaque be placed on her husband and son's favorite campsite and that the name of the island be changed to Happy Isle. Years later, however, when the name appeared on the park map, it was mistaken for the name of the lake (previously called Green Lake for its clear color).

It is obvious why the family had liked the island campsite so much, centered amidst a canopy of stout white pines, with its stone fireplace overlooking the lake high atop a rock outcrop. It was here, after a late dinner, that I sat close to the evening fire and reminisced about the first time I canoed with my father.

It was back in 1976. We flew into a fishing lodge in Ontario's Algoma region, and after spending an entire week trolling unsuccessfully from an aluminum motorboat out on the main lake, my dad and I decided to rent a canoe and portage into a small pond rumored to hold trophy-size trout.

Both of us being first-time canoeists, the long trek in to the remote fishing hole was a bit of an ordeal. But we caught fish, and, in retrospect, I think we discovered the freedom of wilder-ness at the same time.

On day three of my solo trip, keeping with tradition, I portaged the 370 yards (340 m) into Merchant Lake to go fishing. According to Ralph Bice, one of Algonquin's best-known guides, Merchant was long considered one of the best fishing lakes in the park; one of the largest officially recorded lake trout, weighing 34 pounds (15.4 kg), was caught here in the early 1920s by a party from Northway Lodge.

It took me just an hour of trolling, with a silver-and-gold Williams Wobbler, to prove that Merchant Lake hadn't changed. I caught my limit, keeping the smallest to cook up for a late lunch back at the campsite.

After filling up on battered lake trout and greasy home fries smothered in ketchup, I packed up my gear and paddled east to the Opeongo portage. My plan was to finish the portage just before dusk and then paddle over to the nearby site where I had camped on my first night out. But for some reason, after carrying my last load across, I felt like continuing on.

It didn't take long for the sun to set, and the sensation of paddling with more light on the water than on land was unusual. But the wind dropped as the evening began, and the moon came out in full. So I set a heading on my compass, placed the instrument down in front of me, and began the night crossing. Everything was serene. Once again, with the help of my father, I had discovered the freedom of wilderness.

Happy Isle Lake

TIME
2 to 4 days (depending on whether you take the water taxi across Lake Opeongo)

DIFFICULTY
As long as you don't plan to paddle across Lake Opeongo, only novice tripping experience is needed.

PORTAGES
1

LONGEST PORTAGE
2,385 yards (2,180 m)

Booth Lake makes a perfect long-weekend getaway.

Booth Lake

A FEW YEARS BACK I WOULD NEVER HAVE CHOSEN to write up Booth Lake as a prime canoe route. Not that there was anything wrong with the route; with only two short portages it happens to be one of the easiest three-day trips in the park. But until recently, the road leading to the access point was in such poor condition that the route was too difficult for most canoeists to reach. Now, however, a new road has greatly improved access, and the route is one of the best long-weekend getaways Algonquin has to offer.

To reach the access point, turn north off Highway 60 at the village of Madawaska onto Major Lake Road. Then drive for 16 miles (26 km) to the gatehouse located on the right (just before the Opeongo River bridge separates Farm and Crotch Lakes). The put-in is located across the road, to the left of the bridge, and from there the route heads upriver to Farm Lake.

From the weedy entrance to Farm Lake, paddle directly across to rejoin the Opeongo River. Then head upstream again, this time to Kitty Lake. Here, where the river bends to the left, is one of the last remaining ranger cabins in the park.

The Kitty Lake cabin was built in 1935 from older logs salvaged from nearby Booth Farm. Cabins like this were built by the rangers, who, usually former loggers and trappers from the area, would travel from hut to hut to trap nuisance wolves, watch for fire outbreaks, and apprehend poachers — some turning out to be their own partners — in exchange for low wages and bland food.

The bush plane quickly changed the ranger's life in the interior, and by the 1950s the old cabins had become obsolete and were considered fire hazards. Many were burnt to the ground, but a few relatively inaccessible cabins, including the one on Kitty Lake, were left alone.

After visiting the cabin site, paddle to the base of the nearby rapids and either line your canoe up the short swift or take the 100-yard (90 m) portage marked to the left. Continuing upstream, a quick paddle will take you to a second set of rapids and a tougher, 600-yard (550 m) portage marked to the right and leading into Booth Lake.

Exceptional campsites can be found almost anywhere on Booth Lake, but the rock outcrops dominating the left-hand shoreline and a sandy beach stretched out along to the right hold some of my favorites. After making camp, there's still time to head farther west to check out the Preston Tower

Booth Lake

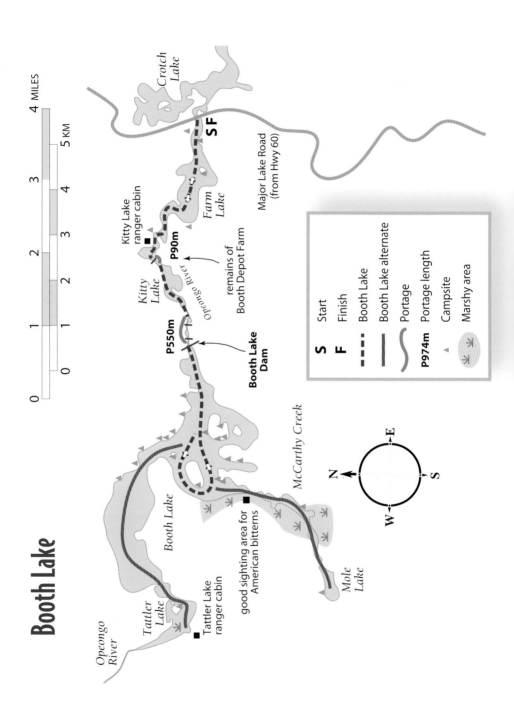

Legend:

S Start
F Finish
Booth Lake
Booth Lake alternate
Portage
P974m Portage length
▲ Campsite
Marshy area

Crotch Lake

S F

Major Lake Road (from Hwy 60)

Kitty Lake ranger cabin

Farm Lake

P90m

remains of Booth Depot Farm

Kitty Lake

Opeongo River

P550m

To Farm Lake

Booth Lake Dam

McCarthy Creek

N E
W S

Booth Lake

Mole Lake

good sighting area for American bitterns

Tattler Lake ranger cabin

Tattler Lake

Opeongo River

0 1 2 3 4 MILES
0 1 2 3 4 5 KM

Cabin on Tattler Lake. Four years younger than the Kitty Lake cabin, the Preston Tower cabin was built to provide lodging for the park ranger who manned the fire tower to the west of Tattler Lake.

You can also take a trip up McCarthy Creek to Mole Lake. The entrance to the marshy creek is located at the southwest corner of Booth Lake, and here, at its mouth, is one of the best places to catch a rare glimpse of an American bittern. Known for its secrecy, the bittern is able to quickly blend in with its surroundings by quickly pointing its bill skyward and stretching out its brown-and-beige-striped neck. If a stiff breeze begins to blow against the stems of cat-tails and bulrushes, the bittern maintains its camouflage by swaying back and forth in time.

It's much easier to locate the bittern by sound. Listen for its springtime song, which has a mechanical rhythm similar to the sound of an old water pump, giving the heron-like bird the nickname "thunder pumper." If you don't happen to hear the bittern's "pump-er-lunk" the first time out, be sure to return to McCarthy Creek just after nightfall, when the birds are more active.

You should think of leaving Booth Lake before noon the next day (the way out is simply the reverse of the way in). As long as your whitewater skills are up to snuff, you can make the return trip much quicker by running the rock-strewn rapids below the Booth Lake dam, as well as the short swift just before the Kitty Lake cabin.

Booth Lake

TIME
2 to 3 days

DIFFICULTY
Novice

PORTAGES
4

LONGEST PORTAGE
600 yards
(550 m)

"How do you eat through this thing?"
(Scott Roberts battles bugs along the Tim River.)

Tim River Loop

AFTER A FEW YEARS OF PADDLING TO BIG TROUT LAKE by way of the Petawawa River (see Upper Petawawa Loop), my regular canoe cronies and I decided to head down the Tim River, which runs parallel to and north of the Petawawa. The trip is a little more rugged, but the portages are less crowded and the fishing is fantastic.

The route heads out from the same access point on Magnetawan Lake. But after carrying over the 150-yard (135 m) portage into Hambone Lake you travel east into Butt Lake by way of a relatively flat 225-yard (295 m) portage.

Butt Lake, one of the deepest lakes in the park, was originally called Eagle Lake (eagles were once thought to nest on the cliff along the south shore). The lake, and the township in which it was located, were named after Isaac Butt, of Dublin, a prominent Irish Nationalist who died in 1879.

The route continues east across the length of Butt Lake into Little Trout Lake by way of a 475-yard (435 m) portage, and then across a flat but muddy 190-yard (175 m) portage into Queer Lake.

My canoemates and I camped on Queer Lake for our first night out. It was a short day on the water, but to chance carrying our gear over the lengthy portage to Tim River, paddle an hour downstream to the only marked campsite near the put-in, and hope to find it vacant, didn't seem logical. Instead, we spent the afternoon exploring the south bay of Queer Lake, casting for trout along the shoreline, and sneaking up on a cow moose and her calf feeding in the shallows.

Knowing we had to paddle the entire length of the Tim River in one day (there are no suitable campsites on the lower stretch) and still wanting to take advantage of the excellent fishing holes en route, we found ourselves at the take-out of the 1,455-yard (1,330 m) portage, located at Queer Lake's northeastern tip, just before 8 a.m.

My canoe partner, Scott Roberts, and I, eager to wet a line at the base of the small falls just upstream from the put-in, jogged across the portage, stopping only to catch our breath at the top of the two steep knolls near the trail's beginning. The plan was that once we finished the portage, Scott would unpack the fishing gear while I loaded the canoe.

In record time I flipped the canoe upright, tossed the packs on both sides of the center thwart, lashed the bow to the trunk of a stout spruce tree, and then trotted over to join my faithful companion directly below the cascade.

Lifting over just one more logjam (Tim River).

The moment I saw my rod and reel tossed in an alder bush, my line tangled in the branches, and my lure box still unopened, I knew I had been had. The scoundrel had failed to keep his side of the bargain, and by the time I geared up, Scott had caught and released three nice-sized brook trout and caused enough commotion in the process to spook the remaining fish in the pool. I was furious and refused to talk to him for at least an hour. But after paddling downstream, casting over Scott's head to get first dibs on the next three holes, and lucking out with my limit of fish, my mood slowly changed.

The first half of the Tim, representative of the river's original name, Pine River, is typified by impressive white pines rooted close to the narrow sandy banks. The second half, however, is totally different. The gentle current reaches out to feel its banks as the river begins to meander uncontrollably through dense alder thickets and patches of leather leaf alive with the songs of the magnolian and yellow-throated warblers. The first two of the river's three portages are halfway along. The first, measuring 300 yards (275 m) and marked to the left, leads through the remnants of the Pine River Farm. The original clearing, used by the Colonial Lumber Company to keep the loggers' horses and to plant vegetables, was over 203 acres (81 hectares). Now a small field located at the take-out and a ranger's cabin built from salvaged lumber in the late 1920s are all that remains of the depot.

Not far downstream, just before the more swampy section of the river, is the second portage. The 505-yard (460 m) trail, also marked on the left, has a steep take-out and follows along the top of an eroded bank.

Eventually, the Tim returns to its original shape, and after the third and final portage, measuring 140 yards (125 m) and marked to the right, the waterway empties out into Shippagew Lake. After a long day on the meandering river, the campsite, situated on a rock outcrop to the east, looked inviting. But Shippagew Lake is far too shallow for trout, and with all of us being fishing fanatics, we agreed to push on and carried our gear up and over the 1,040-yard (950 m) portage into Blue Lake.

We were glad to see that the only campsite on the lake was still unoccupied when we finished the portage, and after pitching our tents, we eagerly jumped back into the canoes to try and catch our dinner — all of us except for Peter, that is. No friend to undue effort, Peter simply impaled a scented rubber minnow on a bare hook, threw it off a rock ledge directly in front of the campsite, and sat back on his Therm-a-Rest lounger waiting patiently for a strike. After an hour of paddling out on the lake, we returned exhausted and empty handed only to find out that Peter had already caught, cleaned and consumed his catch.

We all slept late the next morning, tired from our long day on the Tim. Then, after exiting Blue Lake by way of a rugged 920-yard (840 m) portage, marked at the end of the eastern inlet, we made our way down Big Trout Lake. By noon, our lazy strokes had only taken us to Big Trout Lake's western bay. We stopped for a shore lunch on an island campsite and cooked up a few lake trout we had caught along the way. Peter's fish was the biggest, of course, and he was given the honor of cooking up the catch his way — frying the battered slabs of white meat in a glob of oil. His only mistake

Tim River Loop

TIME
5 days

DIFFICULTY
Moderate

PORTAGES
22

LONGEST PORTAGE
1,455 yards
(1,330 m)

was asking me to lend him a hand when his batter mix ran low. I innocently offered him some flour I found in an unlabeled container stashed away at the bottom of my food pack. Peter poured the contents into the batter, wondering why the mixture wouldn't thicken. It wasn't until he had used up the entire supply that I discovered that the flour was actually coffee whitener. We ate the fish anyway and didn't mention our secret ingredient to the others until two days later when Scott noticed I was drinking my coffee black. Peter snickered, and the jig was up.

After our fish fry out on Big Trout, we paddled into White Trout Lake by way of the western inlet and then made camp near Grassy Bay at the southeastern tip. Now over halfway through our trip, we finally started to develop a routine. During the two days remaining, spent looping back to the access point on Magnetawan Lake by way of the Petawawa River (see Upper Petawawa Loop for a route description), we were completely organized. We had learned to load our canoes with efficiency, and our paddle strokes were in perfect time. During our last evening (spent on Misty Lake), we all grabbed our rods and reels and sat on a rock ledge beside Peter, who, of course, caught the biggest fish again.

Upper Petawawa Loop

THE MOMENT THE ICE IS OUT AND TROUT SEASON IS OPEN, my regular canoemates and I head for the park's interior to endure cold nights, soggy portages, bloodthirsty blackflies, and freak snow-storms, all in the hope of spotting a moose, smelling the sweet aroma of spring flowers, or hooking into a trophy-size trout.

Throughout the years, we've altered our route in search of bigger fish and less-crowded portages. However, we've made the majority of our outings in the west side of the park's 2,955 square miles (7,653 sq km). This lake-covered highland, from which three major rivers flow (the Petawawa, Nipissing and Tim), is a haven for lake trout and pink-fleshed brook trout.

From Access 3 on Magnetawan Lake, a perfect four-to-five-day loop can be had, with the added bonus of avoiding any portage longer than 985 yards (900 m) — something I'm sure that regular park users would agree is hard to come by in Algonquin's interior.

To reach Magnetawan Lake, take Highway 11, north of Huntsville, and make a right onto Highway 518 at Emsdale. Follow 518 to the town of Kearney, and then, keeping left where the road splits, continue for another 8.9 miles (14.4 km) until you reach the graveled Forestry Tower Road. Make a right here, following the rough road for 8.1 miles (13 km) to the MNR Office.

After picking up your interior camping permit, follow the gravel road, keeping to the right, for another 7.6 miles (12.2 km), to the parking area on the northwest shore of Magnetawan Lake.

From the parking lot, a short path leads to the dock on Magnetawan Lake. After you lock up your vehicle and load your gear into the canoe, a quick paddle directly across from the dock will take you to the first portage (150 yards [135 m]) of your trip, leading into Hambone Lake.

Keeping to the right shoreline of Hambone Lake, paddle into the second elongated bay. There, where the waterway narrows, a quick 60-yard (55 m) portage on the left avoids a shallow section. In high water, however, you can usually paddle straight through if the bow person keeps an eye out for hidden rocks.

The channel opens up into a small pond, with the next portage (460 yards [420 m]) marked directly across. The rugged path leads the way to Daisy Lake, working its way over a mountain of rock, and then down to a makeshift dock sunk into smelly swamp ooze.

Peter Fraser catches yet another trophy-sized lake trout.
How one angler can possess such luck is beyond belief.

On Daisy Lake, head south out of the bay and then east toward the sandy shallows where the Petawawa River begins. A 150-yard (135 m) portage to the left is necessary to avoid the place where the river drops over a rock shelf. The river then flows into a narrow, meandering waterway lined with alder, dogwood and patches of tamarack.

Shortly after, another portage (495 yards [450 m]) is marked along the left bank. Some canoeists choose to shorten the carry by paddling the middle section between a set of double rapids. Once the canoe is balanced over my shoulders, however, I prefer to keep going to the bitter end.

Downriver from the put-in of the last portage, the river starts to become less constricted. Eventually it opens up into Little Misty Lake, where you may see some of Algonquin's four thousand moose browsing in the shallows. The number of moose sighted depends greatly on the time of year. On one particular trip, the salt-enriched aquatic plants had just begun to sprout, drawing the moose to the water's edge, and we counted a grand total of twenty-nine moose feeding in the weedy effluent.

The first moose sighting of that same trip was the most memorable. Scott, my canoe partner, and I had stopped paddling for a swig of juice and a handful of GORP while our friends went on ahead. After a few minutes had passed, we decided we had better push on if we were to catch up with the others. Just around the next bend, however, we found our companion's path blocked by an odd-looking moose wading in midstream. The beast refused to move for at least twenty minutes. Of course, the moment I decided to take advantage of the situation and unpack my camera, the moose sprang out of the water and into the bush. Later that same day we overheard some other canoeists telling a similar tale of a half-crazed moose blocking their path at the same spot on the river, except they were able to shoot an entire role of film before the moose stepped aside.

At the far end of Little Misty Lake, the largest portage en route (1,025 yards [935 m]) heads over a steep knoll, carpeted by maple, beech and birch (typical forest cover of the western uplands), to the north-western bay of Misty Lake.

Misty Lake is an excellent spot to make camp for the first night. My favorite site, which is on the north side of the large island, is well protected from the winds that always seem to pick up on Misty, and has an excellent rock outcrop from which you can cast a line for trout cruising the shallows come dusk.

Day two is spent back on the Petawawa en route to Big Trout Lake, the centerpiece of Algonquin's interior. The river flushes out at the end of Misty Lake's elongated eastern inlet. Here you will find an 930-yard (850 m) portage marked to the left, starting up a steep and slippery embankment. Two short sets of rapids, the first with a 170-yard (155 m) portage to the left and the second with a 215-yard (195 m) portage to the right, are also located not far downriver. Of the two, only the first can be run.

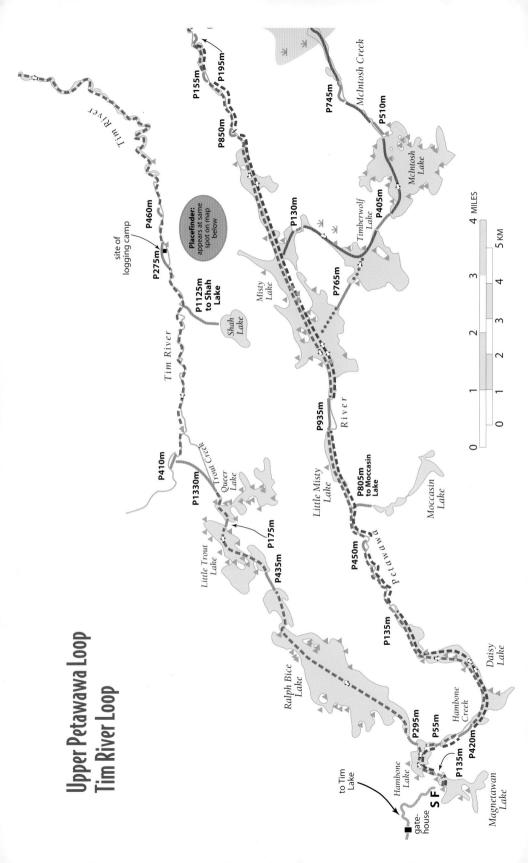

Upper Petawawa Loop
Tim River Loop

P155m
P195m

McIntosh Creek

P850m

P745m

P510m

McIntosh Lake

P130m

Timberwolf Lake

P405m

Tim River

P460m

site of logging camp

P275m

Placefinder: appears at same spot on map below

P1125m to Shah Lake

Shah Lake

Misty Lake

P765m

Tim River

P410m

Trout Creek

P1330m

Queer Lake

Little Trout Lake

P175m

P435m

River

P935m

Little Misty Lake

P805m to Moccasin Lake

Moccasin Lake

P450m

Petawawa

P135m

Ralph Bice Lake

Daisy Lake

Hambone Creek

P295m

P55m

P420m

P135m

Hambone Lake

to Tim Lake

S F

gatehouse

Magnetawan Lake

0   1   2   3   4   MILES

0   1   2   3   4   5   KM

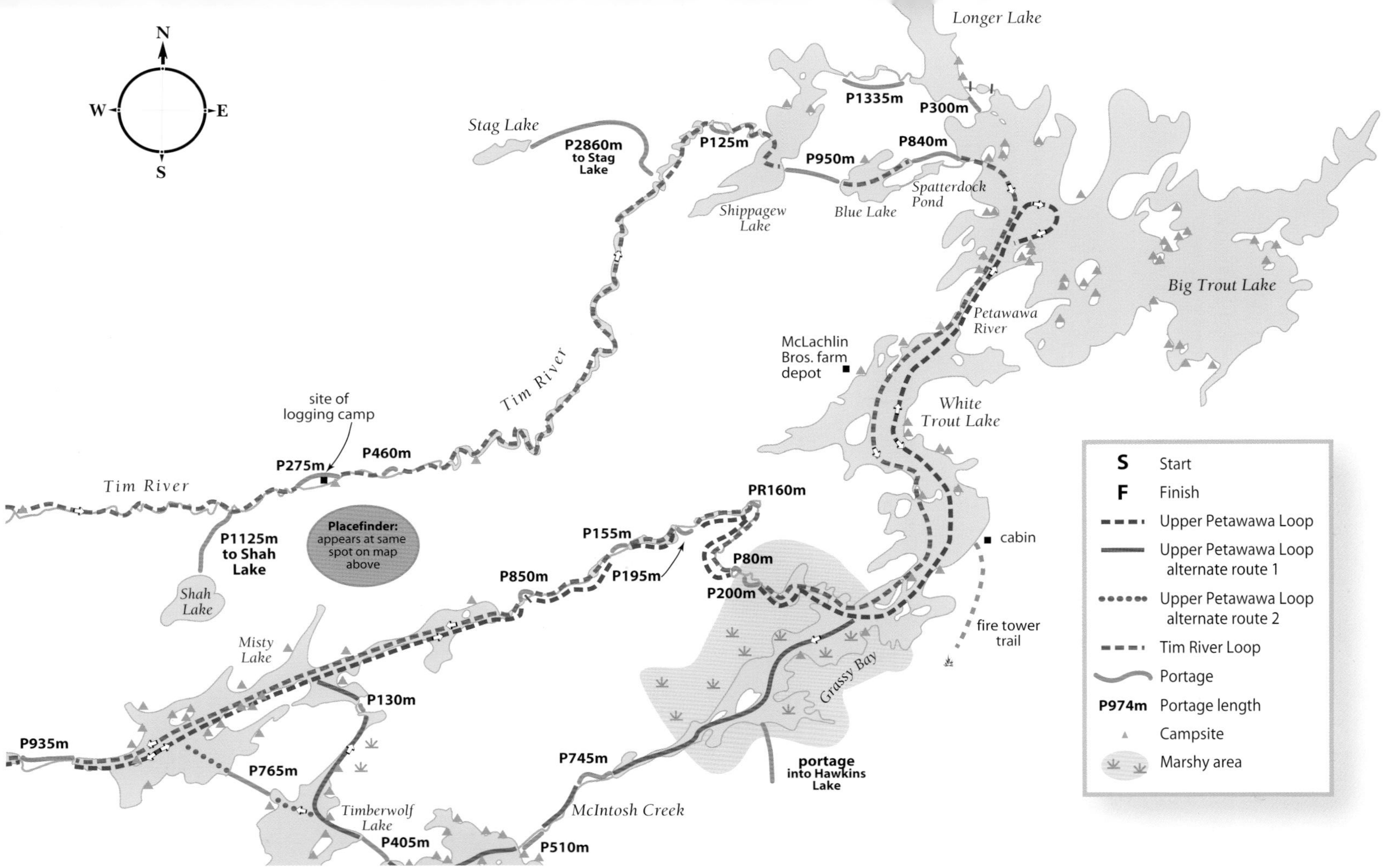

Legend / Map labels:

S Start
F Finish
— — — Upper Petawawa Loop
——— Upper Petawawa Loop alternate route 1
•••••• Upper Petawawa Loop alternate route 2
– – – Tim River Loop
⌒ Portage
P974m Portage length
▲ Campsite
Marshy area

Big Trout Lake
Longer Lake
P300m
P840m
P1335m
P950m
P125m
Spatterdock Pond
Blue Lake
Shippagew Lake
Petawawa River
White Trout Lake
cabin
fire tower trail
McLachlin Bros. farm depot
PR160m
P80m
P200m
P195m
P155m
Grassy Bay
portage into Hawkins Lake
P850m
McIntosh Creek
P745m
P510m
P2860m to Stag Lake
Stag Lake
Tim River
P460m
site of logging camp
P275m
Placefinder: appears at same spot on map above
P1125m to Shah Lake
Shah Lake
P130m
Timberwolf Lake
P405m
Misty Lake
P765m
P935m
Tim River

N
E
S
W

The river once again slows its pace and then takes a sharp turn to the south at a scenic double chute. A steep, 175-yard (160 m) portage on the right heads directly overland, well below the rough water, and you must paddle a good distance upstream from the put-in if you wish to view the base of the run.

High cliffs, with small pockets of white pine growing out of the thick stands of black spruce now begin to interrupt the low, swampy banks. A dramatic falls follows the last cascade of water upriver; there is an 90-yard (80 m) portage to the left. Directly after this, to the right, is a 220-yard (200 m) portage to avoid the last set of rapids of the day, where the Petawawa flows into the swampy shallows of Grassy Bay.

It's become a ritual for me and my canoe companions to cast a line for speckled trout at the base of each rapids along the entire stretch of the Petawawa. If the fish are biting, we're pretty much guaranteed a "brookie" on the first cast. One can imagine, then, the competitive nature of the group as we race over the portage in a race to be the first to fish the hole. My canoe partner, Scott Roberts, has a special knack to beat everyone to the punch. But after he had caught and released over half a dozen good-sized specks, the group decided to allow Mike, who had yet to catch anything on all of our previous trips, to have first dibs on the last hole of the day.

Mike and his canoemate, Doug, pushed off from shore to reach the center of the deep pool. We all stood and watched with anticipation as Mike's lure slapped the surface of the water and then sank beneath the soft current — all of us except for Scott, that is. The scoundrel had grabbed his rod and reel from his pack, sneaked through the brush, and taken a cast from shore.

Before we could protest his unsportsmanlike conduct, both Mike and Scott hooked into a fish. Sadly, however, Mike's bad luck had prevailed. While Scott proudly displayed a two-pound brook trout, Mike was busy wrestling with his lure, which had deeply embedded itself into his catch — a slimy sucker!

From the base of the last rapids, head out into the twisting channel of Grassy Bay, which eventually splits east and west. Head east into the expanse of White Trout Lake and either make camp here, or paddle across and through the connecting channel to Big Trout Lake. Big Trout has count-less island campsites, but in the past our group has chosen always to camp on the smaller White Trout Lake, spending an entire day exploring the old McLachlin farming depot used by loggers in the early 1900s or hiking up to the site of the abandoned fire tower. The farm post can be found along the shore to the northeast, and the tower trail begins at the south end of White Trout Lake, where a ranger cabin can be sighted in a clearing. The tower has been recently dismantled by park staff for safety reasons, but the one-and-a-half-hour hike to the peak is still worthwhile.

After a rest day exploring White Trout Lake or fishing for monster lake trout on Big Trout Lake, the next two days are spent looping back to the access point on Magnetawan Lake. To return, enter back into the swampy maze of Grassy Bay from White Trout Lake's southeastern tip, and instead of paddling up the Petawawa River, head directly west into the main channel of the labyrinth.

Even with provincial park signs posted on stumps to point the right way through Grassy Bay, it's not difficult to find yourself questioning your whereabouts every ten minutes. With every channel looking the same, you will probably end up unpacking your map and compass now and then to locate the main throughway to McIntosh Creek.

Grassy Bay and McIntosh Creek join by way of a 815-yard (745 m) portage, crisscrossing the creek along its entire length. You must lift over a number of beaver dams before you reach a second portage. This 560-yard (510 m) path climbs out of the lowlands and up into McIntosh Lake.

From McIntosh's northwestern bay, a 445-yard (405 m) portage connects you with Timberwolf Lake (an excellent spot for lake trout). And finally, to get back to Misty Lake from Timberwolf, choose either to take a soggy 840-yard (765 m) portage located at the north end or paddle northeast up a weedy inlet to a shorter, 145-yard (130 m) portage.

The loop ends on Misty Lake, where you will spend your last night in Algonquin's interior. The rest of the route retraces itself back up the Petawawa River to Daisy Lake, and then north to Hambone and west to the Magnetawan access point.

Upper Petawawa Loop

TIME
4 to 5 days

DIFFICULTY
Moderate to novice

PORTAGES
22

LONGEST PORTAGE
1,025 yards (935 m)

Rain Lake access offers a number of quick and relatively easy canoe route options into Algonquin's east end.

Misty Lake Loop

I HADN'T USED THE RAIN LAKE ACCESS POINT that much when I first started paddling Algonquin. I'm not sure why. It might have something to do with a nightmarish Fall trip I did into McCraney Lake where low water made McCraney Creek almost impassable. Or maybe it's because the Magnetawan and Tim Lake access points to the north always seemed to have more options for canoe trips. Whatever the reason, I thought I'd give the Rain Lake access another try and headed out on a solo trip in early September.

Getting there couldn't be any easier. I picked up my permit in the town of Kearney at the Park Office (located in the Kearney Community Center). At Emsdale on Highway 11, I turned right and followed Highway 518 for 5 miles (8 km) to reach Kearney. From there it was just a short distance down the main street where I made a left (past the liquor store) to Rain Lake. It's 15 miles (24.5 km) to the access point, most of it on a gravel washboard road.

Rain Lake was once a bustling place. In 1895 the old Ottawa, Arnprior and Parry Sound Railway passed straight through, making it an excellent place to set up lumber mills. The Brennan Lumber Company located their mill first, followed by J.R. Booth Lumber Company, Canadian Woods Products and then Muskoka Wood. One of the first cottages in the area was also built on Rain Lake. Charles Waterhouse, owner of Deerhurst Lodge in Peninsula Lake, had it built in 1925 as an outpost for fisherman. A few more camps were put up, one on the island in 1937, and a few more, including one by the family of well-known author and Algonquin trapper, Ralph Bice. Soon it became a poplar spot to start a canoe trip and the park established "Eagle Lake Landing" to process campers and anglers going into the park.

Rain Lake access also doubles as an entry point for the Western Uplands Hiking Trail, which now uses a portion of the abandoned railway line. One route option I thought of doing originally was to loop through Islet and McCraney to the south for a few days and use a portion of the hiking trail as a day outing. However, I wasn't yet over the bad memories I had of McCraney Creek. So I decided to head east towards Misty for five days, looping through a series of smaller lakes.

It was raining when I began crossing Rain Lake. Fitting I guess. The lake itself was first titled Rainy Lake by an old-time trapper, Jake Clancy, who named it after dealing with constant rain storms on the lake. Rainy Lake was changed to Rain Lake soon after the railway arrived due to too many

letters and parcels at the post office arriving here rather than Rainy Lake in Western Ontario.

At least the drizzle kept the winds down to a minimum. Rain Lake seems more like a wide river at times than an actual lake and I can imagine winds can become quite harsh running down its length. It still took me an hour-and-a-half to make the crossing, stopping once to gawk at an immature bald eagle shifting its wings back and forth as it caught a thermal of warm air high above the lake. What an amazing site.

Misty morning on Misty Lake — it doesn't get any better than this.

The first portage, leading to Sawyer Lake, was short by Algonquin standards. It measured only 340 yards (310 m) and besides a boulder covered take-out, the trail was pretty easy to navigate. The campsites looked a little over used, however. Similar to the ones on Rain Lake. I'm guessing these two lakes see a lot of weekend abuse and I was glad to be heading deeper into the park before making camp.

The next portage (600 yard, 550m) into Jubilee Lake was longer and tougher — littered with small rocks and outcropped roots. And at the put-in

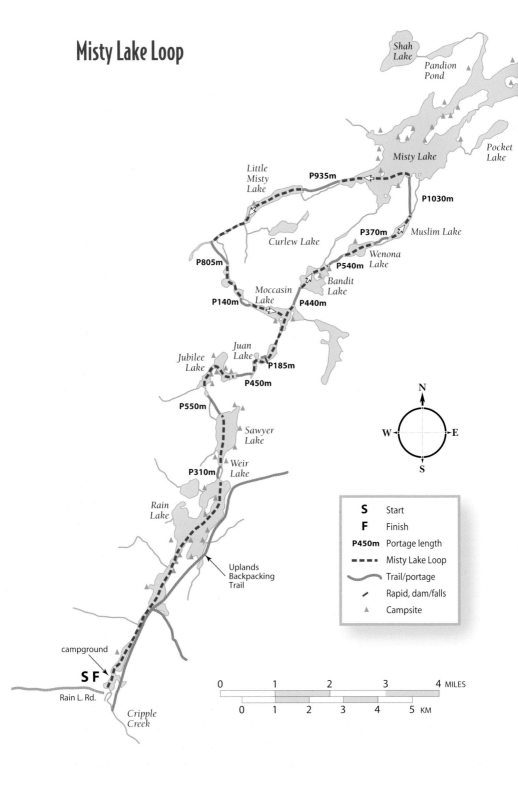

Misty Lake Loop

Shah Lake

Pandion Pond

Misty Lake

Pocket Lake

Little Misty Lake

P935m

P1030m

P370m

Muslim Lake

Curlew Lake

P540m

Wenona Lake

P805m

Bandit Lake

Moccasin Lake

P440m

P140m

Juan Lake

Jubilee Lake

P185m

P450m

P550m

Sawyer Lake

Weir Lake

P310m

Rain Lake

Uplands Backpacking Trail

	S	Start
	F	Finish
	P450m	Portage length
	- - - -	Misty Lake Loop
	‿	Trail/portage
	╱	Rapid, dam/falls
	▲	Campsite

N

W — E

S

campground

S F

Rain L. Rd.

Cripple Creek

0   1   2   3   4 MILES

0   1   2   3   4   5 KM

I had to wade through some shallow marshy bits before the canoe was able to float freely. But still, it wasn't a bad portage compared to others in the park. It was the next one (490 yards, 450 m) taking me into Juan Lake — where things got a little tougher. The trail was also full of rocks and roots, but as an added bonus it had a number of short hills to scramble up and over on, plus a boggy section complete with rotting planks to walk across. It was impossible to get to the other side without getting both feet wet.

The last portage of the day was just as rough but much shorter — only 200 yards (185 m) to Moccasin Lake. The lake looks more like a pond at first but soon it opened up to a larger piece of water and I took the first of two campsites on the lake. Both were unoccupied and I ended up having the entire lake to myself that night and went to sleep to the sounds of a barred owl making the familiar "who-cooks-for-you, who-cooks-for-you-all" only a few meters from my tent.

Moccasin Lake marked the beginning and ending of the loop section of the trip and in the morning of the second day I had to make the decision to go the Misty Lake clockwise or counterclockwise. I was told the portages were more downhill if I went counterclockwise but that would mean paddling upriver on the Petawawa River section. From past trips I knew that section of river really had no current to be concerned with, so I opted for counterclockwise.

I spent the second day of the trip carrying over four portages and paddling across three small lakes (Bandit, Wenona and Muslim) to reach my final destination — Misty Lake. The first portage (480 yards 440 m) exited Moccasin Lake at the elbow of the small southeastern inlet. It resembled the rough trails I did at the end of day one. So did the second portage. The 590 yards (540 m) had some good muddy sections to wade through and a couple of small trees blocking the route to negotiate around. The 405 yards (370 m) into Muslim was fine. Great actually. And then came the last 1126 yards (1030 m) into Misty. That wasn't bad either. It was long, but the trail went downhill most of the way and had the least amount of mud holes.

It was only mid-afternoon when I reached Misty Lake but I knew going further would only get me to Little Misty before dark. So I had planned on making it an early second day to take some time to explore one of the best lakes of the route. I've traveled this lake a lot while traveling other routes out from the Magnetawan access, and one of my favorite sites is on the northwest corner of the large island. The only problem I have with Misty Lake is I don't usually catch many trout here. On this trip I spent the afternoon trolling the edges of the lake. I ended up, however, eating Mac and

An advantage of solo tripping is that you don't have to deal with a tent mate that snores too much.

Cheese for dinner that night; my substitute when the fish don't cooperate. But I still had a nice lazy afternoon of paddling and trolling a lure behind me.

My lack of fish was soon forgotten when the wolves starting howling just after dark. What an amazing experience to be sitting alone around a small campfire and be serenaded by a pack of wolves. I'm guessing they were the howls of Algonquin's notable Red or Eastern Wolf.

Recently, the wolves in Algonquin park have been reclassified, and by doing so, have gained extra protection. It was always thought that the wolves in Algonquin were distinct and somewhat different from the typical Grey Wolf (*Canis lupus*) of Ontario's more northern boreal forests. They certainly look different; being much smaller and having a reddish-brown texture to their fur. Researchers dating back to the 1970s thought they were a subspecies of the Grey Wolf and they were labeled *Canis lupus lycaon*. Soon a number of biologists began disputing the connection to the Grey Wolf and believed they were more closely related to the highly endangered Red Wolf (*Canis rufus*) of the southeastern United States. Many others debated the distinction. The endangered labeling would give the Algonquin wolves more protection against hunting and trapping and some interest groups didn't want that to happen. In 2000, however, DNA testing became available and members of the Algonquin Wolf Advisory Group were able to reclassify them as the Eastern Canadian Wolf (*Canis lycaon*). The debate was over.

Recently other Eastern Wolves have been found in areas neighboring Algonquin (Kawartha Highlands Provincial Park for example) and some areas of Quebec, Manitoba and Minnesota. Algonquin's wolves, however, are thought to be the purest strain since they have not interbred with coyotes to the degree the others have. The reason for this, of course, is that coyotes do well in urbanized areas; wolves don't. As long as Algonquin remains relatively wild, so will the wolves.

I could feel the change in weather while crawling out of the tent on the third morning of the trip. The days of August had slipped by and autumn had crept in during the night. The air was crisp and the temperature cool. You could even see a few deciduous leaves starting to change color. I welcomed the change. Autumn is my favorite time to paddle in Algonquin. There's less people, no bugs, and the scenery is incredible. It was good to get on the move and warm up a bit by covering the 1022-yard (935 m) portage leaving the northwest corner of Misty to Little Misty. The trail, beginning to the right of where the Petawawa River flushes into Misty Lake, has a steep knob of rock to climb up and over, and a few wet spots to walk through.

Grass and sedge began lining the banks where the Petawawa River joins the west side of Little Misty. It's not a true river here, meaning there's no strong current to push against while traveling upstream. Besides, it didn't take long before the route turned off the river and headed south. Here, an 880-yard (805 m) portage took me back in the direction of the familiar Moccasin Lake. Two signs marked the portage, the first is where you paddle through a clump of marsh to get to the take-out and the other directly where you unload the canoe. The trail leads to an unnamed lake and comes complete with an abrupt hill near the beginning and more mud holes to wade through.

The unnamed lake is actually an extension of the north arm of Moccasin Lake and is blocked by some downed trees, looking like some giant game

Misty Lake Loop

TIME
4–5 days

DIFFICULTY
Moderate level
of experience
needed

PORTAGES
15

**LONGEST
PORTAGE**
1,126 yards
(1,030 m)

of pick-up-sticks. With the little use that the 153-yard (140 m) portage (marked to the right) had received, I guessed that the labyrinth of logs and branches can be navigated through in good water levels. At the time, however, it seemed easier to just get out and portage.

I decided on a change of pace and rather than camp on Moccasin Lake again, I continued on through Juan and Jubilee to camp on Sawyer, using the familiar 200-yard (185 m), 490-yard (450 m) and 600-yard (550 m) portages. Sawyer is a nice lake, and it also allowed me to get out onto Rain Lake early my last morning to beat the prevailing winds that can make Rain Lake difficult for a solo canoeist.

There to serenade me once again for my last night out were one of the thirty packs of Eastern Wolves that call Algonquin home. This time they were closer to my camp than they were when I was camped on Misty Lake. And this time it was a series of higher pitched barks and yelps that seemed to go on for well over an hour. I guessed it was a kill a few had made and then had decided to call on all the others to check out. I listened along the lake shore until I began to shiver, then reluctantly went to the tent, zipped up tight inside my sleeping bag and dozed off dreaming of my next late Autumn canoe trip to Algonquin.

Kingscote/Scorch Lake

SOMETIMES THE BEST PLACES TO PADDLE ARE RIGHT in your own backyard. Algonquin Park's Kingscote/Scorch Lake route is a great example. I paddle Algonquin a lot. Most of my trips there, however, start off from the north end, even though the southern access is just over an hour's drive away from my home in Peterborough. I'm not sure why I commonly ignore the more easy-to-get-to routes. Maybe it's because most paddlers think that the best places to travel are usually the most difficult to reach — which is most likely true, except when it comes to Algonquin's Scorch Lake. Its scenic splendor equals or even surpasses the majority of the park's more northern routes.

To reach the access, take Highway 648, 1 mile (1.6 km) east of the village of Harcourt. Follow the Elephant Lake Road north for 7.5 miles (12 km) and before turning left into the Kingscote Lake Road, pick up your permit at Pine Grove Point Lodge and Campground on your right. Then, go back to the Kingscote Lake Road and keep to that road for 4.4 miles (7 km) and turn right to the access point.

Kingscote is a relatively new access point for Algonquin Park. Historically, there was a cottage housed here, but in 1999–2000, under the Living Legacy Program, the Nature Conservancy of Canada helped Ontario Parks purchase and develop a mini campground at the south end of Kingscote. I've stayed at the campground and quite enjoyed the less-crowded drive-in or walk-in sites. The area boasts some incredible mountain-bike trails and a prime hiking trail along the York River. However, I much prefer paddling further into the interior, north of Kingscote.

The area gained more protection due to the famous Kingscote "silver" lake trout. The trout differ from the common lake trout found throughout Algonquin by their uniform body color devoid of the common white spots or vermiculations. It's quite an amazing story, actually. These native subspecies of lake trout have somehow survived six decades of supplemental stocking. Basically, the local fish have adapted and outdone the captive species. It's a clear sign of biodiversity — something that desperately needs to be protected. Over time, Kingscote Lake has reduced its "cold water" habitat, and with it the high oxygen content. Rather than dying off, however, these trout adapted to the changing habitat. Some fisheries experts have compared this to the difference between aurora trout and brook trout. It's a rarity for sure.

A few prime campsites exist on Kingscote, especially on the far northeastern shoreline. In general, it's not a busy lake, even though 20-horsepower motors are still allowed. However, I found that the majority of campsites on the lake were overly shaded in among a thick canopy of cedar.

The group I paddled with on the last outing, film friends Kip Spidell and Ashley McBride, was able to get to the access point early, and we were across Kingscote Lake by mid-morning.

The first portage of our trip was a lengthy one. It measures 1,422 yards (1,300 m) and leads to Big Rock Lake. About a quarter of the way along, another trail forked to the left, leading to Lower and Upper Minnow lakes — both providing fair brook trout fishing. The rest of the trail to Big Rock had more than a few wet spots along the way and ended with a marshy stretch where it was impossible to keep our feet dry. And to add to the punishment, a good hill had to be dealt with near the end as well.

Most of Big Rock Lake is to the south, but our route went north and it wasn't a long paddle up to the top of Big Rock Lake before we reached the next portage. The Big Rock to Byers Lake portage measured 722 yards (660 m) and had a good downhill slope to contend with (and an uphill slope to contend with on our return). It was here we stopped for lunch — a site that was good enough to stay the night at, but we had planned on going all the way to Scorch Lake, so we continued on up the York River.

Here, the York River resembles a small lake and it's unnoticeable that you're on a river after leaving Byers Lake. Our group even second-guessed our whereabouts at one point due to Branch Lake looking more like a widening of York River than an actual lake. The good news, however, is that we lucked out on the way up the York by coming across a bull moose grazing in a marshy bay.

It took a good chunk of paddling for us to reach the portage leading to Scorch Lake. Scorch Lake is a real gem. We camped at a great site, on a rocky point toward the southeast corner of the lake. We were also the only ones there for the two days we base camped — a rarity in busy Algonquin Park. Our site even overlooked Scorch Lake Mountain, which we planned to ascend the next day.

We had an early supper and went to bed the moment it got dark. It had been a long day en route to Scorch Lake, a trip that should have been attempted in two short days rather than one long one. But by pushing all the way to Scorch Lake, we had a full day to climb the summit trail and overlook the incredible landscape we had traveled through to get there.

After a breakfast of flapjacks, bacon and a double dose of strong coffee, we all headed to the southeast corner of the lake to begin the hike to the top

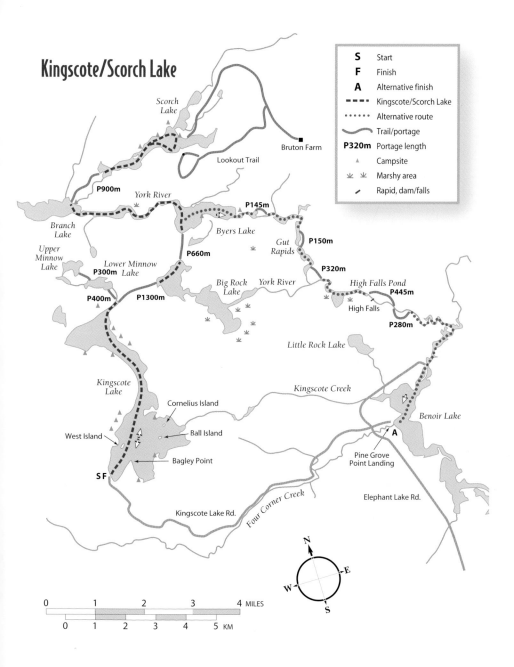

Kingscote/Scorch Lake

Scorch Lake

Bruton Farm

Lookout Trail

P900m

York River

P145m

Branch Lake

Byers Lake

Gut Rapids

P150m

Upper Minnow Lake

Lower Minnow Lake

P660m

P320m

P300m

High Falls Pond

P400m

P1300m

Big Rock Lake

York River

P445m

High Falls

P280m

Little Rock Lake

Kingscote Creek

Kingscote Lake

Cornelius Island

Benoir Lake

West Island

Ball Island

A

Bagley Point

Pine Grove Point Landing

SF

Elephant Lake Rd.

Kingscote Lake Rd.

Four Corner Creek

S	Start
F	Finish
A	Alternative finish
- - -	Kingscote/Scorch Lake
· · · · ·	Alternative route
⌒	Trail/portage
P320m	Portage length
▲	Campsite
⸎ ⸎	Marshy area
⸍	Rapid, dam/falls

N
W — E
S

0	1	2	3	4 MILES
0	1	2	3 4	5 KM

of Scorch Lake Mountain. The trailhead was easily found, tucked away in the far corner of the bay. Before taking the main path to the peak, we kept left where the trail forked and visited the old Bruton Farm. It wasn't a long hike and took us through some mature stands of maple and beech. An old stone fence marked the beginning of the old homestead and the forest trail continued across a logging road to the centerpiece of the farm. Not much was left of the farmhouse, four barns, blacksmith's shop and numerous

*The view from the top of Scorch Lake Mountain
is the highlight of the trip.*

smaller outbuildings, but it was an intriguing place and a good excuse to hike through some prime hardwood.

On our return we scrambled up the mountain trail, which went straight up a steep slope almost immediately and ended up on top with a moderate loop circling the crest. The viewing platform was a simple slab of rock covered in slippery moss. This was obviously not a well-visited spot.

Kingscote/Scorch Lake

TIME
2–3 days

DIFFICULTY
This is an easy trip except for a couple of long portages where some canoe-tripping skills would be an asset.

PORTAGES
6

LONGEST PORTAGE
1,420 yards (1,300 m)

The view was definitely worth the 0.6 miles (1 km) climb, but hordes of biting blackflies shortened our stay. We had returned to camp by late afternoon and all agreed that Kingscote/Scorch Lake makes up one of the best nearby paddle routes Algonquin has to offer.

High Falls, Nipissing River.

Nipissing Loop

IT WAS MID-AUGUST 1995, AND ALANA AND I, eager to explore the isolated stretch of the Nipissing River between Allen Rapids and High Falls, had planned an extensive ten-day loop out from the Kawawaymog Lake (Round Lake) access point. It was the first time we had visited the north end of the park. The moment Alana and I entered the wood-framed gatehouse, we noticed that the walls and counter tops were cluttered with snapshots — some of park wildlife, others of park regulars holding up record-breaking lake trout. The attendant, dressed in a wrinkled uniform and bright pink baseball cap, greeted us as long-lost relatives, and before leaving with our interior permit we were given a detailed commentary on every photo on display.

The warm welcome we received at the gatehouse that day helped set the mood for the rest of the trip — one of the best routes Algonquin has to offer.

To reach the Kawawaymog access point, located just outside the park's western border, turn east off Highway 11 on Ottawa Avenue, in South River. A 14-mile (22 km) drive down a gravel road takes you to the parking area and gatehouse.

From the government docks, the route heads east. Cross the lake by following the left-hand shoreline. Next, travel down the Amable du Fond River, which marks the entry point to the park and links Kawawaymog Lake with North Tea Lake. This stretch of river is approximately two-and-a-half miles (4 km) long, and winds its way through tamarack swamp decorated with flowering pickerel weed and prickly rose.

Halfway along, the river splits. To the north, a narrow creek empties out of Pat Lake. Keep to the main route, which continues east. Soon after the fork, the river begins to straighten out; cedar and spruce take over the swamp tamarack, and lily pads grow out toward the center of the waterway.

Two portages (150 and 280 yards [135 and 255 m]) are marked in succession just before the Amable du Fond River flows into North Tea Lake. This section can become quite busy. Alana and I were unaware of North Tea's popularity, and upon reaching the second portage, were shocked to see over a dozen beached canoes, their occupants all contending for room for their packs along the shore. We waited a good twenty minutes, and then, eager to escape the crowded take-out, we leapt out of the canoe and unloaded in midstream. I flipped the canoe onto my shoulders and then had to step over a spilled cooler of beer, fight off an unleashed yappy poodle, maneuver around an obese lady collapsed with exhaustion, and

Nipissing River Loop

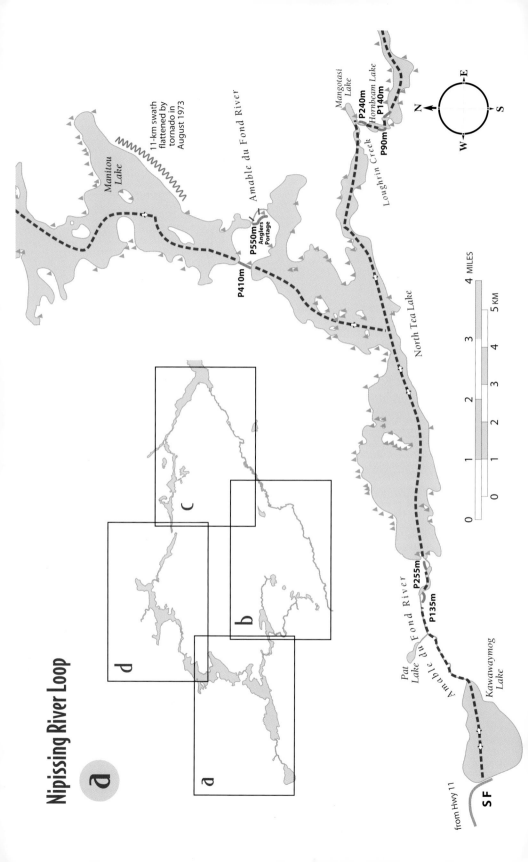

S F

from Hwy 11

Kawawaymog
Lake

Amable du Fond River

Lake du Fond River

Pat
Lake

P135m

P255m

North Tea Lake

Loughrin Creek

P90m

Hornbeam Lake

P140m

P240m

Mangotasi
Lake

P410m

P550m
Anglers
Portage

Amable du Fond River

Manitou
Lake

11-km swath
flattened by
tornado in
August 1973

a

b

c

d

N
W   E
S

0   1   2   3   4 MILES

0   1   2   3
5 KM

b

Nadine Lake

P1410m to Nadine Lake

cabin site

1930m portage to Remona Lake

P850m

P1300m

High Falls

cabin ruins

P365m

P495m

Nipissing River

P2715m

Allen Rapids

Legend:
- **S** Start
- **F** Finish
- - - - Nipissing River Loop
- ——— Nipissing River Loop alternate route
- ∿∿ Portage
- **P974m** Portage length
- ▲ Campsite
- ⚮ Marshy area

Birchcliffe Lake

cabin

P1395m

Calm Lake

P1020m

P260m

Birchcliffe Creek

P120m

Lawren Harris Lake

cabin

P20m

Loughrin Lake

P640m

JEH MacDonald Lake

P495m

P10m

P1950m

P345m

Biggar Lake

P2010m

osprey nest

P495m

Barred Owl Lake

P10m

Nod Lake

P1950m

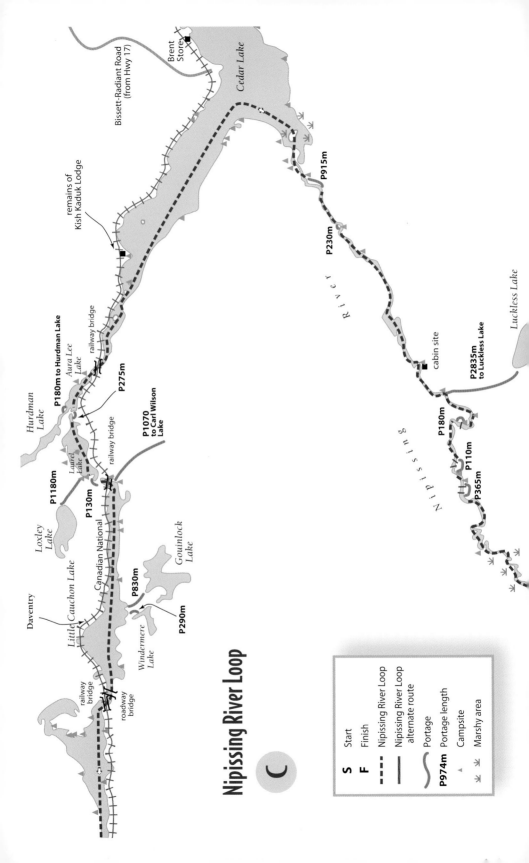

Nipissing River Loop

Legend:

- **S** Start
- **F** Finish
- Nipissing River Loop
- Nipissing River Loop alternate route
- Portage
- **P974m** Portage length
- Campsite
- Marshy area

Brent Store

Bissett-Radiant Road (from Hwy 17)

Cedar Lake

remains of Kish Kaduk Lodge

P915m

P230m

River

Luckless Lake

cabin site

P2835m to Luckless Lake

P180m

P110m

P365m

Nipissing

railway bridge

P180m to Hurdman Lake

Hurdman Lake

Aura Lee Lake

P275m

P1180m

Laurel Lake

P1070 to Carl Wilson Lake

railway bridge

P130m

Loxley Lake

Canadian National

Gouinlock Lake

P830m

P290m

Windermere Lake

Daventry

Little Cauchon Lake

railway bridge

roadway bridge

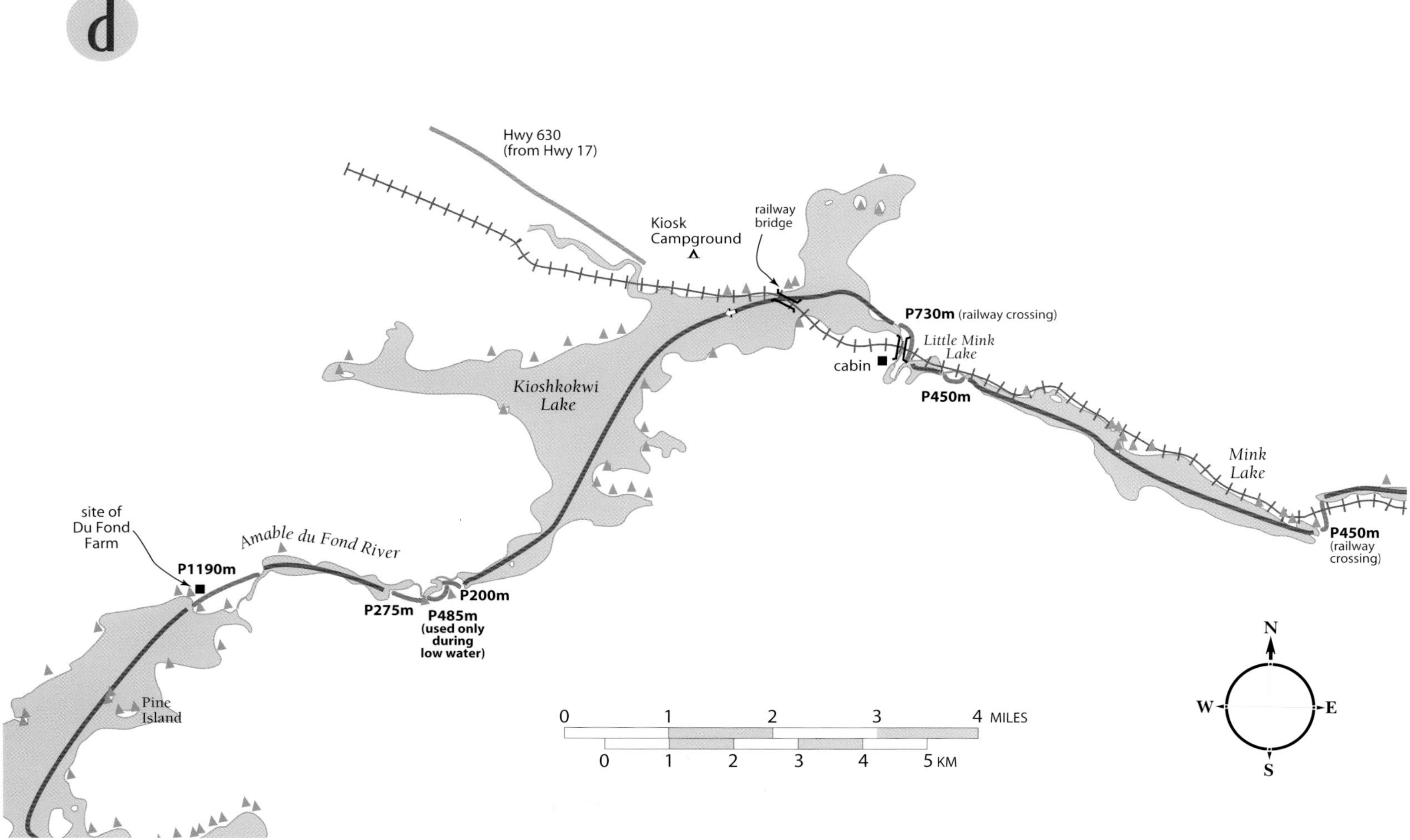

P

Hwy 630
(from Hwy 17)

Kiosk
Campground

railway
bridge

P730m (railway crossing)

Little Mink
Lake

P450m

cabin

Mink
Lake

P450m
(railway
crossing)

Kioshkokwi
Lake

P200m

P485m
(used only
during
low water)

P275m

Amable du Fond River

P1190m

site of
Du Fond
Farm

Pine
Island

N
W E
S

0   1   2   3   4 MILES

0 1 2 3 4 5 KM

interrupt two teenage lovers making out just off the trail, before I finally reached the put-in.

We checked out the historic plaque commemorating F. X. Robichaud and Tom Wattie, two park rangers working in the area during the early 1900s. (Robichaud died alone in his cabin on nearby Three Mile Lake.) Then, wading out past another jumble of canoes, we paddled out into the expanse of North Tea, where the crowd eventually thinned out.

The route heads across North Tea and into the eastern inlet. Near the end of the inlet (Mangotasi Lake on map A), a series of three portages (265, 100 and 155 yards [240, 90 and 140 m]) are marked along the stream flowing out of Biggar Lake. The first and third portages are along the left bank, and the second is marked to the right of a stunted cascade that tumbles down into a small pond called Hornbeam Lake. Take note that the section between the second and third portage can become a rock garden if water levels are low.

Biggar Lake is a good place to camp for your first night out. The campsites on the west end, tucked away behind strands of heavily browsed cedar, are disappointing. But farther east, a number of prime tent sites are marked atop rock outcrops, directly opposite a breathtaking rock face, near the mouth of Loughrin Creek.

From Biggar Lake, the route heads south to the Nipissing River by way of either Loughrin or Birchcliffe Creek. Some canoeists choose to wade up the sandy-bottomed Birchcliffe Creek provided water levels are low, as Loughrin can become a horrific mud bath. This will take you past the old ranger's cabin on the southwest shore of Birchcliffe Lake (see map for details). In general, though, Loughrin Creek is a more direct route, with swampy sections providing excellent opportunities to spot moose.

The entrance to Loughrin Creek is at the south end of Biggar's central bay. A short paddle up the creek takes you to the first portage along the narrow stream. This 2,200-yard (2,010 m) trail, marked to the left, is relatively flat at first. Halfway along, however, two steep slopes slow your progress to a snail's pace. At the base of the second hill, the path meets back up with the creek and follows it along for a good distance, passing under gigantic white pine rooted along the bank.

From the put-in, the creek twists and turns through a wide stretch of swamp and eventually narrows at a stand of black spruce. Here, you're forced to drag the canoe over abandoned beaver dams and jagged rocks to the next portage — an easy 700 yards (640 m) across a logging road and into Lawren Harris Lake (named after the Group of Seven member, who painted in the park between 1914 and 1916).

At the south end of Lawren Harris Lake are the remains of an old ranger's cabin. The roof caved in a few years back, and now young birch and aspen trees have sprouted up through the center of the weathered shack.

The route continues into Loughrin Lake over a 22-yard (20 m) portage, which passes near the cabin and to the left of a logjam. It then heads to the southwestern inlet, where a 540-yard (495 m) portage takes you over a steep rise leading to Barred Owl Lake. Directly across from the put-in is a short lift-over into Nod Lake, and then, to the south, a 2,135-yard (1,950 m) portage takes you to the tea-colored water of the Nipissing River. The trail is lengthy, but relatively flat, except near the put-in, where it makes a dramatic turn to the left and heads up a steep slope.

A campsite is marked at the end of the 2,135-yard (1,950 m) portage. It's a poor site, though, and when Alana and I reached the spot, we decided to push on downstream to camp at the end of the 380-yard (345 m) portage marked to the left of a rustic dam. Chilled from a long day of paddling and portaging in the rain, we cooked up a quick supper and headed into the tent early, with mugs of hot cocoa and a deck of cards. Three games of cribbage later, the cocoa kicked in and we both had to go out for a pee. When we unzipped the front tent flap, however, we came face to kneecap with a gigantic bull moose standing directly beside our flimsy nylon tent, browsing on the alder thicket on which our wet clothes hung to dry. For the sake of our bladders, we quietly slipped out the back flap. On our return, the only evidence of our visitor was a steaming moose patty blocking the entrance to the tent and a pair of socks missing from the alder bush.

We were on the river early the next morning, slowly drifting under the immense pines that spread out over the narrow waterway. By the time the hot sun chased off the looming mist, we could began to hear the rush of Allen Rapids.

This stretch of rock-strewn rapids could probably be run, with care; the only problem is that it's impossible to scout from the 2,970-yard (2,715 m) portage that runs along the left bank. Your best bet is to carry your gear three-quarters of the way down the trail, up to where a campsite is marked along the river. From there to the designated put-in is a series of simple swifts that can be easily navigated.

Approximately two hours downstream from Allen Rapids are two more portages (540 and 400 yards [495 and 365 m]). The first is marked to the right of a scenic falls, and the second, equipped with a steep gravel slope at the take-out, is marked to the left and leads through a field littered with the remnants of several cabins left over from the logging era. The river spreads

Sun and sand on Manitou Lake.

itself out from here, the soft current sifting through sedge and bulrush before eventually being pinched between canyon walls and tumbling over the twin ledges of High Falls.

The 1,420-yard (1,300 m) High Falls portage, marked to the left, follows dangerously close to the cascade and has a steep take-out. With the rugged terrain comes a magnificent view, especially halfway along the trail. A picture-perfect campsite, situated on the south shore, is available at the base of the falls.

Downstream from High Falls, the river briefly stretches out again and then makes a dramatic turn north before another stretch of white water. Portages are marked on both sides of the river here. Be sure to take the 930-yard (850 m) trail located along the left bank.

Once past the trail leading into Nadine Lake, the river heads east again and begins to meander uncontrollably through spruce lowlands. From here it takes approximately three-and-a-half hours to reach the next series of portages. The first two (400 and 120 yards [365 and 110 m]) are marked to the right, and farther downstream, the third portage (200 yards [180 m]) is marked to the left. One or two campsites are marked at each portage, but none compare to the scenic spots upstream at High Falls, which you should consider if you find yourself at the falls late in the afternoon.

What remains of the Nipissing before Cedar Lake is more of an elongated lake than a gurgling river, with only two portages not far upstream from the river's mouth. The first (250 yards [230 m]) is to the left of a runnable swift, and the second (1,000 yards [915 m]) is to the right of an old logging dam.

A weedy delta marks the end of your journey down the Nipissing, its pine-clad banks and tea-colored water quickly being replaced by the expanse of Cedar Lake. To celebrate your arrival at the halfway mark, a trip to the Brent Store, situated directly across from the river's mouth, is in order.

Alana and I, after stuffing ourselves with junk food, continued north on Cedar Lake for another hour and then made camp at the site adjacent to the ruins of the Kish-Kaduk Lodge. The resort was first opened by Mr. E. Thomas in 1928, and up until a few years ago the buildings remained relatively intact. Sadly, however, the historic site has frequently been used for parties (note the assortment of beer cans in the basement), and the neglected lodge has become quite an eyesore. But the campsite is not bad; just watch out for broken glass and rusty cans when walking in the back-woods or wading in for a swim.

The morning mist had long since lifted from the surface of Cedar Lake by the time Alana and I started up again in the morning. We were sluggish from our diet of chips and pop the day before, but our efficiency out on the water was restored by the time we entered Cedar Lake. A shallow channel clogged by islands and half-submerged logs marks the entrance to the first of the series of connecting lakes that would take us back across the park.

After a quick paddle across Little Cedar Lake, the route continues up a shallow creek and under a cement railway bridge to Aura Lee Lake. The crossing is the first of six spots where the route travels either under or over the now-abandoned CN line. The last train came through here on November 25, 1995, thanks mostly to the dedicated opposition of the Canadian Wildlands League. But our trip was four months before the clos-ing date; so Alana and I were forced to put up with this noisy intrusion to the park's environment (mind you, both of us, after cursing the noise of the locomotive as it passed by, still instinctively waved at the conductor like a couple of schoolchildren).

There are two portages marked at the far end of Aura Lee Lake. Keep close to the left-hand shoreline and take the 300-yard (275 m) trail that exits into Laurel Lake. Once across Laurel, continue to the left and take the steep, 140-yard (130 m) portage into Little Cauchon Lake, marked to the right of a picturesque cascade.

A two-hour paddle up Little Cauchon and Cauchon Lakes, and an easy, 480-yard (440 m) portage remain before you make camp on Mink Lake. Before the closure of the CN line, I would have been hard pressed to

Snack break at the Brent Store.

recommend camping on Mink Lake or any of the other nearby adjoining lakes. The majority of the sites are uncomfortably close to the track, and when Alana and I stayed here overnight, our tent shook every time a train went by. But now Mink Lake offers somewhat secluded campsites. Take note, however, that the area's bothersome red squirrel population can still make your life miserable. These critters have the dexterity to clamber down onto your suspended food pack, tear it apart, and then raid the stash of munchies you purchased back at the Brent Store.

The next day, two portages (495 and 800 yards [450 and 730 m]) take you to the eastern end of Kioshkokwi Lake (*kioshkokwi* is Algonquin for "gull"). From the weedy put-in, stay close to the left-hand shoreline until you come to the last railway bridge en route. Once you reach the opposite end of the trestle, a 4-mile (6 km) paddle west across the expanse of Kioshkokwi Lake will take you to the first of a double set of rapids at the base of the Amable du Fond River.

The ease of the trip upstream depends highly on water levels. In normal conditions, a series of three portages (220 and 300 yards [200 and 275 m], marked to the left, and a surprisingly easy 1,300 yards [1,190 m], marked to the right) takes you directly into Manitou Lake. During a dry spell, however, an extended 530-yard (485 m) portage, marked between the first and second portages, may be necessary.

Near the end of the last portage, just before walking onto the sandy beach at the put-in, you'll come across what little remains of the once-thriving Dufond Farm, now almost totally taken over by a gigantic patch of wild raspberries. Ignace and Francis du Fond, two descendants of the Indian chief Map di Fong, who hunted here during the early 1800s, established a farm on the north end of Manitou some time during the 1880s. The settlement was the last and only deeded farmland in the region (usually only timber rights could be secured). They made a healthy living selling fresh produce to local lumber companies, and Ignace's wife, nicknamed Old Susanne, is frequently praised in the rangers' journals for her excellent meals and good nature — except for the time she served a roasted groundhog, head and all.

The winds on Manitou can be treacherous; so, when Alana and I reached the lake and found it to be surprisingly calm, we took full advantage. We paddled to the southernmost end, portaged over the steep 450-yard (410 m) portage into North Tea Lake, and finally called it quits on the first island campsite. It was an extremely long day on the water, but the next day, when we awoke at five o'clock in the morning to a stiff breeze building from the east, the extra hours of easy paddling seemed well worth the trouble.

In twenty minutes, Alana and I had the canoe loaded. We raced toward the west end of the lake, being chased all the way by ever-increasing winds. We felt safe once we reached the small river heading back to the access point, and at the take-out we decided we were due for our morning coffee; so, under a torrential downpour, we over-turned the canoe, stuck one end up in the crook of a tree, and huddled underneath the makeshift shelter to light the camp stove. I was just about to balance the pot of water over the blue flames, however, when Alana caught sight of a large group of canoeists coming toward us. Remembering the stampede mentality of the horde of people we met on the same portage on our way in, we canceled our coffee break and made a run for it, chased this time not by gale-force winds, but by a massive herd of Algonquinites.

Nipissing Loop

TIME
8 to 10 days

DIFFICULTY
Due to the length of this route and the long portages along the way (especially on the upper Nipissing River), moderate to high tripping experience is needed.

PORTAGES
33

LONGEST PORTAGE
2,970 yards (2,715 m)

Spending some quality quiet time (Maple Lake).

Erables Lake

JOHN BUCK AND I TOGETHER HAVE BEEN PLAGUED by bad luck. In 1994, while paddling down the remote White River in Pukaskwa National Park, our entire party was severely food poisoned by a can of toxic oysters. Then, during a trip along the isolated Lake Superior coastline a year later, a new member of our group, Grace, came very close to dying of a strangulated hernia. Being wise to the old wives' tale that bad things happen in threes, I had to make absolutely sure that our next adven-ture was a simple one. Algonquin's Erables Lake immediately came to mind.

The route's access point is on the north shore of Kioshkokwi Lake. To reach the put-in, turn south off Highway 17 onto Highway 630 and follow the 19-mile (30 km) stretch of paved road to the Kiosk campground. The campground is an excellent place to spend your first night if you arrive late in the day, and the launch site is directly across from the campground's office and parking lot.

On our first day out, we enjoyed a leisurely pace. From the access point, we crossed the width of Kioshkokwi Lake, and hugging the southern shore-line, we headed west. Eventually we reached the mouth of the second large bay and paddled up to the base of Maple Creek, where six steep portages lead up to Maple Lake.

The first portage (850 yards [775 m]) is one of the toughest climbs. To make matters worse, the take-out is on the opposite side of the creek during low water conditions, making it impossible to keep your feet dry before slogging your way up the steep bank.

Next is a long stretch of creek with the odd beaver dam to lift over and then a shorter, easier portage measuring 210 yards (190 m) and marked to the left. Here, near the put-in, a side trail leading into a raspberry patch to the left takes you to the site of an old logging camp. Although little remains — two dozen rusted metal bunks and the rotted outline of the building that once housed them — the fresh raspberries along the trail make the side trip well worth the effort.

The creek snakes its way along again before the remaining portages (100, 690, 880 and 140 yards [90, 630, 805 and 130 m]) follow in quick succes-sion. Of the four, the 690-yard (the only portage marked to the right) and the 880-yard portage are the most difficult.

Once on Maple Lake, we paddled south out of the long bay and then directly across to the twin islands to the south. Then, just to the left of the

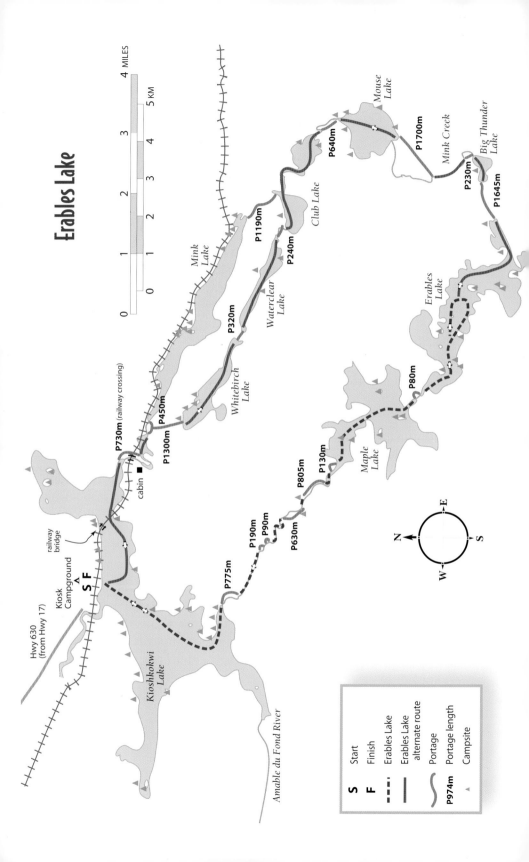

Erables Lake

4 MILES

5 KM

Mouse Lake

P640m

P1700m

Mink Creek

Big Thunder Lake

P230m

P1645m

Mink Lake

P1190m

Club Lake

P320m

P240m

Waterclear Lake

Whitebirch Lake

P450m

P730m (railway crossing)

P1300m

cabin ■

Erables Lake

P80m

railway bridge

Kiosk Campground

S F

P190m

P90m

P130m

P775m

P805m

P630m

Maple Lake

Hwy 630 (from Hwy 17)

Kioshkokwi Lake

Amable du Fond River

N E S W

S Start
F Finish

——— Erables Lake

– – – Erables Lake alternate route

〜 Portage

⌒ Portage length

P974m Portage length

▲ Campsite

islands, we found the entrance to the weedy creek that joins Maple Lake with Erables Lake (*erables* is French for "maples"). A short distance up the creek, a 90-yard (80 m) portage, crossing a well-used logging road, took us into the more scenic of the two lakes. We made camp on the first of the two island campsites.

Many canoeists continue on from Erables and loop back to Kioshkokwi by way of Mouse and Mink Lakes. In order to avoid the two long and relatively steep portages en route, however, we decided to spend both nights camped on Erables. From here, we spent a rest day photographing moose feeding at the mouth of Maple Creek, to the south, and fished the depths of the lake for its trophy lake trout.

On the third day, John and I headed back down Maple Creek to Kioshkokwi Lake. Then, just as we were about to lift over one last beaver dam, a sharp rock hidden in a pile of branches, slashed open the side of our flimsy canoe.

We panicked at first; after all, we still had the rough waters of Kioshkokwi Lake to contend with. But, after our two previous trips, we were prepared for anything. With a single roll of duct tape we were able to fight off this third catastrophe. Our next trip was bound to be a good one.

Erables Lake

TIME
2 to 3 days

DIFFICULTY
Novice (watch the winds out on Kiosk Lake)

PORTAGES
14

LONGEST PORTAGE
880 yards (805 m)

"The last step is a doozy." (Barron Canyon)

Barron Canyon

THE BARRON RIVER, NAMED AFTER AUGUSTUS BARRON, A member of the House of Commons, is clearly the gem of Algonquin Park's east side. The waterway is lined with steep walls of hard, crystalline rock that tower far above the water (300 feet [100 m] at their highest point), isolating the river and helping to defend its solitude.

The cliffs — sculpted by the waters of historic Lake Algonquin some eleven thousand years ago, toward the end of the last Ice Age — dominate the primitive landscape. It took only a few centuries for the incredible volume of glacial meltwater, once equivalent to a thousand Niagara Falls, to retreat northward, from what geologists labeled the Fossmill Outlet, to a lower geological fault — the Lake Nipissing-Mattawa channel — reducing the Barron River to a mere trickle.

To reach the canyon (Access Point 22 on the Algonquin Park map), turn left off Highway 17 (approximately 6 miles [9 km] west of Pembroke) onto County Road 26. Then, after 330 yards (300 m), take the first right at the Achray Road and drive 16 miles (26 km) to Sand Lake Gate, at the park boundary. Once you have received your interior camping permit (you may want to phone ahead to reserve), continue for another 12 miles (19 km) and make a left on a side road leading to the Achray Campground on the southeast tip of Grand Lake. On your way to Achray, you may want to make a quick stop at the Barron Canyon Trail (5 miles [8 km] before the turnoff to the Achray Campground). The one-mile (1.5 km) loop trail provides an excellent view — from the canyon's north rim — of your planned route.

If you arrive late in the day, the campground on Grand Lake is an excellent place to spend your first night, and if time permits, after dinner you can take a quick paddle to the east end of the lake to explore one of Tom Thomson's sketching sites.

In 1916, a year before the famed Canadian artist mysteriously drowned on Algonquin's Canoe Lake, Thomson painted a gloomy jack pine on the small point of land to the left. The conifer had been scarred by fire when Thomson painted it, but managed to stand until the late 1970s, when it finally toppled to the ground and was used for firewood by a group of campers.

Head out from the Achray Campground and portage 35 yards (30 m) in to Stratton Lake. Then, after paddling the full length of Stratton, portage 50 yards (45 m) into St. Andrews Lake. It's best to set up a base camp here

Barron Canyon

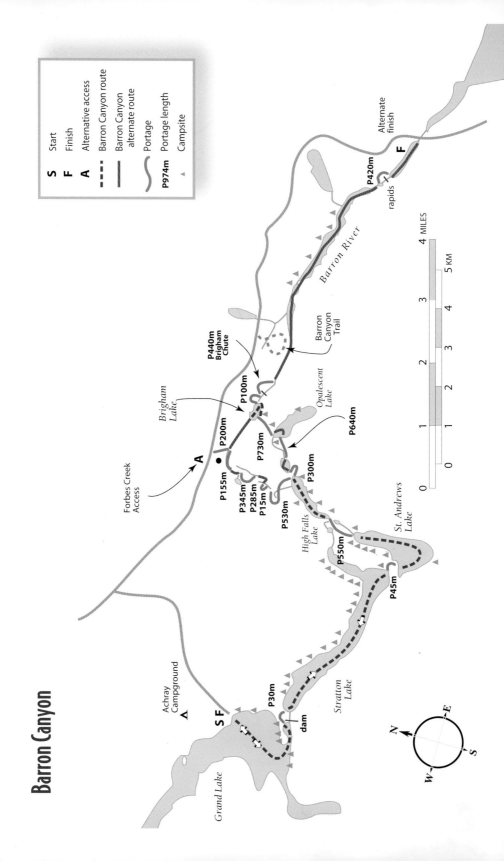

Start — S
Finish — F
Alternative access — A
Barron Canyon route
Barron Canyon alternate route
Portage
Portage length — P974m
Campsite — ▲

Grand Lake

Achray Campground ▲

S F

P30m

dam

Stratton Lake

High Falls Lake

P550m

P45m

St. Andrews Lake

P530m

P300m

P15m
P285m
P345m

P730m

P640m

Opalescent Lake

P155m

A

Forbes Creek Access

P200m

Brigham Lake

P100m

P440m
Brigham Chute

Barron Canyon Trail

Barron River

P420m

rapids

F

Alternate finish

N
W — E
S

0   1   2   3   4 MILES

0   1   2   3   4   5 KM

and then make the visit to the Barron River Canyon in a daytrip.

To reach the canyon from St. Andrews Lake, take the 600-yard (550 m) portage into High Falls Lake. The trail is marked in St. Andrews' northeastern bay. From the northern tip of High Falls Lake, stay with the river by following the 580-yard (530 m) portage to the left. Six more portages (the longest being 380 yards [345 m], and all marked on the left bank except the fifth) lead you into Brigham Lake. Directly across the small pond, two more portages are marked to the left (110 and 480 yards [100 and 440 m]), taking you around the Brigham Chute.

What lies ahead is spectacular: precipitous cliffs, with bright orange lichen (xanthoria) and lime-loving encrusted saxifrage rooted in the damp seepage areas. The canyon appears primeval, and it is easy to imagine that you have traveled back in geological time.

From here, the river is in no great hurry, and you can drift slowly between the granite walls, following the soaring ravens and red-tailed hawks that nest high up on the rock cliffs. When it's time to head back to base camp, rather than lugging your canoe up the sequence of cascades, take the 800-yard (730 m) portage, on the southwestern shore of Brigham Lake, in to Opalescent Lake. Then head directly across to a 700-yard (640 m) portage, followed by a short 330-yard (300 m) portage, to reach High Falls Lake.

Once back at St. Andrews Lake, bake some biscuits, brew up a pot of camp coffee, and gather around the evening fire to rekindle the day's events.

Barron Canyon

TIME
2 to 3 days

DIFFICULTY
Novice

PORTAGES
19

LONGEST PORTAGE
800 yards
(730 m)

It's Hugh's turn to carry the canoe, on the portage between Maryjane Lake and Kawawaymog Lake.

South River

JUST AS THE OXTONGUE RIVER WAS USED AS the main access to Algonquin Provincial Park before the 1930s, the South River was the primary exit. As far back as 1903, outdoor writer James Edmund Jones, while including suggested canoe trips in his book *Canoeing and Camping*, added a chapter "From Dwight to South River." Then, in 1915, painter Tom Thomson ended his first extensive trip through Algonquin by way of the South River (where along the way he supposedly met up with the legendary Grey Owl and cooked him doughnuts). And in 1926, when Camp Pathfinder began extending their canoe outings further afield, the South River train station quickly became a way for the youth camp to get back to their home base at the bottom end of the park.

Throughout the years, however, Algonquin gained a number of easier take-out points and canoeists quickly abandoned the South River route — until recently, that is. In the spring of 2000, Terry Graham, owner of Canadian Wilderness Trips, re-cut a series of portages once used to link Kawawaymog Lake with the river itself. The next season, after hearing about his work on the historic route, I headed up to give it a try.

Originally, my intention was to retrace that exact route by beginning from Terry's base camp on the west shore of Kawawaymog Lake, portaging through the "rediscovered" trails, and then paddling down to the town by the lower half of the South River. Not necessarily wanting to organize a car shuttle, I decided on a possible circle route instead. From Kawawaymog I would head east into Algonquin Provincial Park and then loop back by making use of a series of small lakes and the upper section of the South River, then reconnect with Kawawaymog Lake by traveling north on the old portages.

Agreeing to join me on the trip was canoe mate Hugh Banks, a fellow instructor at Sir Sanford Fleming College, and Boris Swidersky, editor of *Bushwacker* magazine. Hugh had already accompanied me on a number of exploratory routes, and Boris was looking for more content for his "off-trail" periodical, so we made a perfect team. Thus on the first Saturday in June, when water levels were high and the bug population was even higher, we headed off for the unknown.

To reach the Kawawaymog access point, located just outside Algonquin's western border, we turned east off Highway 11 onto Ottawa Avenue, in South River. A 14-mile (22 km) drive down a gravel road led us to the park

South River

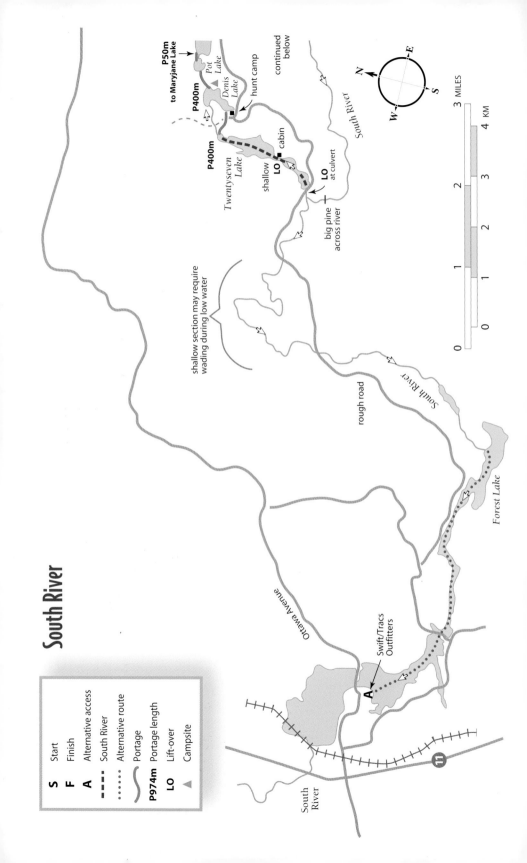

Legend

S	Start
F	Finish
A	Alternative access
	South River
	Alternative route
	Portage
P974m	Portage length
LO	Lift-over
▲	Campsite

P50m
to Maryjane Lake

P400m

Pot Lake

Denis Lake

hunt camp

continued below

Twentyseven Lake

P400m

shallow

LO cabin

LO at culvert

big pine across river

South River

shallow section may require wading during low water

rough road

South River

Forest Lake

Ottawa Avenue

Swift/Tracs Outfitters

A

South River

N
E
W
S

3 MILES

4 KM

0   1   2   3

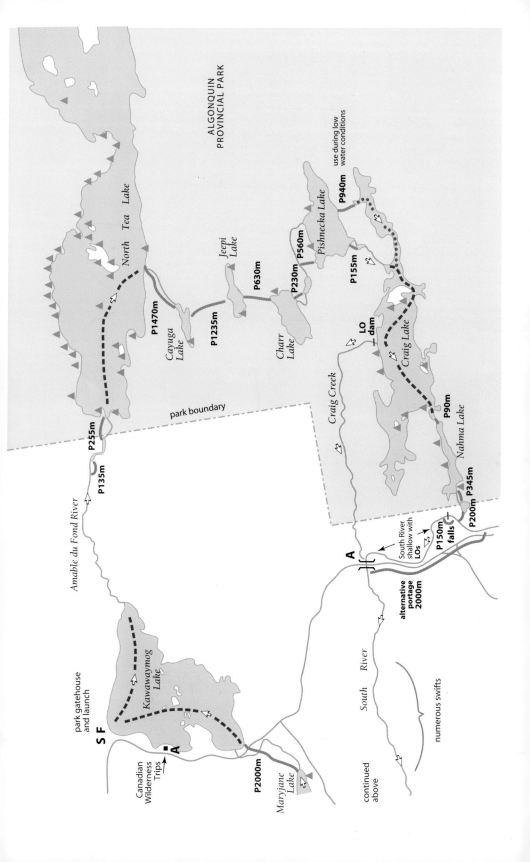

ALGONQUIN
PROVINCIAL PARK

use during low
water conditions

P940m

North   Tea   Lake

Jeepi
Lake

P560m

P630m

P230m

Pishnecka Lake

P1470m

P1235m

P155m

Cayuga
Lake

Charr
Lake

LO
dam

P255m

Craig Lake

P135m

park boundary

Craig Creek

P90m

Nahma Lake

Amable du Fond River

P345m

P200m

P150m
falls

South River shallow with
LOs

A

alternative
portage 2000m

park gatehouse
and launch

S F

Kawawaymog   Lake

South   River

Canadian
Wilderness
Trips

A

numerous swifts

P2000m

Maryjane Lake

continued
above

Boris boils up afternoon tea on his homemade one-burner woodstove.

gatehouse, where we picked up our permit for the two nights we would need to stay in the park.

The usual put-in is directly beside the gatehouse. We all agreed, however, that Terry's camp, situated only a couple more minutes down the road, would make a better place to begin and end our trip.

From the camp we paddled east, passing the same cluster of islands where painter Tom Thomson used to spend time looking over his work — including *Chill November*, *Sand Hill* and *The West Wind* — after returning from one of his sketching trips in the park. Notably, he would spread out his work, keeping only a few paintings, and then give what remained to his friend and park ranger, Tom Wattie, to either keep or burn. (Wattie later remarked that the sketch boards made a brilliantly colored bonfire.)

From the islands we headed to the Amble du Fond River, located on the far northeast corner of Kawawaymog Lake. The river, which marks the entrance into Algonquin Provincial Park, meanders uncontrollably for more than two-and-a-half miles (4 km) and has two portages (a 150-yard [135 m] to the right and a 280-yard [255 m] to the left) near the entrance to North Tea Lake. With a strong east wind blowing across North Tea, it was midday before we found ourselves at the take-out for the portage (1,610 yards [1,470 m]) leading into Cayuga Lake.

After dealing with the heavy winds on North Tea, we were glad to be on dry land — until the bugs found us. A good mixture of blackflies and mosquitoes attacked by the thousands. Instantly we took to the portage, only to find more bugs waiting for us on the trail. And what a trail it was. The long distance was challenging enough. But a steep hill near the take-out and four mud-filled creek crossings were added on for good measure. The portage took almost two hours to complete and it was 7 p.m. by the time we paddled out into Cayuga Lake.

Our initial plan was to camp on Jeepi Lake, which is connected to Cayuga Lake by a lengthy 1,350-yard (1,235 m) portage. Since it was so late, however, we made the group decision to break park rules (you must stay on the designated lake stated on your permit) and stop on Cayuga. The three of us weren't too concerned about camping illegally, since there was little chance for another group to arrive on the lake that night. What did bother us, however, was that we were already behind schedule and were becoming completely exhausted and we hadn't even reached the unmaintained section of the route.

To help keep to our agenda we packed up and headed for the Jeepi Lake portage at dawn. The 1,350-yard (1,235 m) trail was far worse than the previous portage into Cayuga. It had no muddy creeks to step across but the bug's population had doubled along the trail and a total of four steep inclines made the carry an exhausting ordeal.

Sadly, only a five-minute paddle across Jeepi Lake brought us to another lengthy portage, this time along a 690-yard (630 m) trail to Charr Lake. It was somewhat easier, though, with only one hill halfway along. And the next portage, 250 yards (230 m) long and marked to the left of where a creek flows into Charr Lake, was completely flat.

Then, after a short paddle up a marshy stream, we negotiated another relatively flat and easy 610-yard (560 m) portage (marked to the right of where the waterway begins to open up) into Pishnecka Lake.

Obviously, things were looking up. To end our second day, we had only to carry over into Craig Lake. There were two options: paddle southeast across Pishnecka Lake and follow a 1,030-yard (940 m) portage up and over a steep knoll, or keep to the right-hand shoreline and portage only 170 yards (155 m) to where a shallow creek leads into Craig Lake. The difficult 1,030-yard (940 m) portage was used when the creek was unnavigable due to low water. Luckily a heavy rainstorm the night before had kept water levels high and we were able to paddle down the stream quite easily.

By 2 p.m. Hugh, Boris and I found ourselves relaxing on a prime campsite, adjacent to the Craig Lake dam.

In hindsight, we should have continued on for at least another hour or so. Our park permit was for Craig Lake, though. The dam also marked the spot where we had to choose our route to the South River, either portaging around the dam to Craig Creek or paddling east across Craig and Nahma Lakes.

Terry had suggested Craig Creek. He had never been on the upper section of the South River, between Nahma Lake and the confluence of Craig Creek itself, but thought it might be too shallow. Craig Creek also had a number of gravel swifts that would make things interesting, as long as the dam was kept open, of course. But as luck would have it, the dam was closed shut when we arrived.

It was a tough choice: a dried-up creek bed or an unknown section of river that might also be dried up. But the South River was not dam controlled, and so because of the constant rain we had received during the previous couple of days, we opted for the secondary route.

Anxious about what lay ahead, we were again up early, looking for the portage into Nahma Lake. The 100-yard (90 m) trail was located to the southwest on Craig, tucked out of the way in a small lagoon.

From here we paddled across Nahma Lake and made two more consecutive portages (375 yards [345 m] and 220 yards [200 m]) in and out of a small pond.

At the put-in of the last portage we finally met up with the South River. Here again, we had two choices: paddle upstream to begin portaging north along a dirt road for over a mile (2 km) or head downstream and hope for an easy ride down to the confluence of the South River and Craig Creek.

After deliberating over a midmorning snack of jujubes and GORP, we decided on the downstream run. Seconds later, we were halted by a double cascade. The waterfall wasn't a complete surprise to us, since the topo map did indicate some drop in elevation here. It was the idea of pushing our way through the overgrown portage marked on the left that made us rethink our decision. It was only 165 yards (150 m) long, but there were enough trees fallen across it that we wondered if we would ever get to the other side

Not wanting to portage along a lengthy road, however, we kept with the river route. It took us a good half-hour to drag everything through the insignificant trail, but things went quite smoothly after that. The downstream run, from the falls to the confluence of Craig Creek, was small but navigable with only a couple of fallen trees to lift over, a few swifts to maneuver through, and some tight spots where alders grew thick along the bank. Mind you, it would've been a totally different story if water levels had been down.

Once we passed under a bridge, not far downstream from where Craig Creek flushes in from the east, the river widened its banks considerably. The quick current remained, however, and for a good 3 miles (5 km) we enjoyed countless swifts. It was an impressive run. Even the sections between rapids were pretty and serene, the current continuing to hurry along, but without real effort, past massive pine left over from the logging days.

The lumbermen cut the prime white pine mostly off Trout Creek and the South River flats about 1889 and drove them down to Lake Nipissing each spring. The best quality trees were made into square timber, while many lesser quality pine were left untouched. These are the ones that remain along the banks, and they're magnificent.

A number of rock sluiceways were also noticeable along the way, which allowed our group to maneuver down most of the shallow sections of the river without getting our feet wet. Originally the small rock-piles were constructed by the men working for 19th-century lumber baron J. R. Booth; park wardens patrolling the river for poachers continued to maintain them until the early to mid-1900s.

Limbo contestants Hugh and Boris make their way under a logjam on the South River.

The current eventually slowed down around the halfway mark, and we soon came upon a few logjams that had to be lifted over as we continued downriver. Eventually, by 3:30 p.m., we reached where the route headed north. Here, after pulling over a giant pine log, we paddled for another fifteen minutes and then turned right, entering a side channel leading to a metal culvert placed under a dirt road. This ended our trip on the South River and marked the beginning of our journey along the historic portages leading back to Kawawaymog Lake.

We had to get out and wade here and, rather than portage directly over the road, decided to simply walk straight through the culvert. From here we entered the south bay of Twentyseven Lake. The lake, locally and appropriately known as Clear Lake, is divided into two sections by a shallow creek. There was barely enough water to paddle through at the time, so once again we had to get out and wade.

It was a little unnerving to be out of the canoe here. Rumor had it that the owner of the cabin on the north end absolutely detested anyone coming so close to his property. He even had a homemade potato gun resting on top of an old cannon mount, pointing directly at the creek. Lucky for us, however, there was no one on guard while we passed through, and after quickly wading by, we made haste up the lake.

It was our plan that day to make camp on the top end of Twentyseven Lake rather than clear a bush site along the South River. As it happened, the river would have been a better choice. There was no designated campsite anywhere on the lake — not even a bit of flat shoreline big enough for a single tent.

The decision was then made to continue on to Denis Lake (formerly Henry Lake) — our second bad resolution of the day. First, the take-out of the 435-yard (400 m) trail, located on the northeast corner of Twentyseven Lake, was less than obvious. The put-in was also out of sight, up a dirt road to the right and behind a hunt camp. After all that, it was quite late by the time we started searching the shoreline for any possible place to camp. By 7 p.m. we found ourselves set up on a clearing on the far end of the lake. There was no firepit or tent pad, just an open area back in the bush that had been used the previous winter by a local dogsled company. We did our best to practice low-impact camping, making it difficult to even notice that we had ever stayed there.

We were up early the next morning, desperately searching for the whereabouts of the second "lost" portage, a 435-yard (400 m) trail leading into Pot Lake. Terry, the outfitter back on Kawawaymog Lake, had told us that we first had to walk across a wet, grassy area at the far east end of Denis Lake before reaching the take-out. The three of us scattered ourselves along the shoreline and spent half an hour searching. But it wasn't until Boris wandered back toward our campsite, at the extreme corner of the marsh, that he noticed the faint path leading into the woods.

From Pot Lake to Maryjane Lake there was only a quick 55-yard (50 m) portage to the left of a creek. However, the next portage, from Maryjane Lake back to the familiar Kawawaymog Lake, also found to the left of another creek, was a complete nightmare. A makeshift portage sign, the first we had noticed outside the park, was the only positive thing about the extensive 2,185-yard (2,000 m) trail. The first quarter was plagued by steep hills and the last quarter cursed with boot-sucking mud. And in between was an indefinite path blocked with fallen trees and obscured by various side trails. On the first trip over, Boris, who was in the lead, had to pull out his compass four times to confirm that we were at least traveling in the right direction.

It took us two hours to carry everything over to where a road cuts across

South River

TIME
2–3 days

DIFFICULTY

No experience
is required
running rapids
but at least
intermediate
skills are
necessary
because
the route is
physically
demanding.
The alternative
route is rated
as a novice trip,
however.

PORTAGES
16

**LONGEST
PORTAGE**
2,185 yards
(2,000 m)

the portage (the trail picks up again 22 yards [20 m] to the right for the final 220 yards [200 m]). In hindsight, we should have paid more attention to James Edmund Jones's 1903 guide. He suggested back then that canoeists should obtain a wagon and take the tote road from Clear Lake (Twentyseven Lake) to Round Lake (Kawawaymog Lake). Even Tom Thomson cheated at times by hitching a ride back on the neighboring log-train operated by the Standard Chemical Company in the town of South River.

But then again, if we'd avoided the series of lakes between Kawawaymog Lake and the South River we would have missed out on some incredible scenery. We also would never have spotted an osprey nest on Denis Lake or Maryjane Lake or watched a family of otter swimming across Pot Lake. And the sight of the impressive old-growth rooted alongside the portages, especially rare stands of maple and yellow birch, was well worth our efforts. Better yet, we were all able to step back in time for a while, to travel a route that was once a regular thoroughfare and is now left in complete obscurity — which is something all canoeists would agree is a rarity in this day and age.

Lower Petawawa River

THE VELOCITY OF THE LOWER PETAWAWA MORE THAN makes up for the fact that this wild river is Algonquin's only major whitewater trip. It took our group — Dave, Peter, Scott and me — a few years of running lesser rivers before our skills were up to snuff for what the Algonquins referred to as "a noise heard from far away."

The Petawawa originates at Algonquin's west end. But the lower stretch, which holds the most intimidating whitewater, lies between Cedar and McManus Lakes — a trip that takes at least seven days to complete. As intermediate paddlers, the four of us chose only to navigate the shorter stretch between lakes Travers and McManus. The car shuttle is less time consuming, the rapids are less technical, a majority of the portages can be avoided with moderate whitewater experience and good judgment (except in high water conditions), and the trip fits nicely into a three-day weekend.

Before putting in at Lake Travers, you must first drive a second vehicle to the route's end. From Highway 17, turn left onto County Road 26 (approximately 6 miles [9 km] west of Pembroke). Then, after 330 yards (300 m), take the first right at the Achray Road and drive 16 miles (26 km) to Sand Lake Gate, at the park boundary. Once you have picked up your interior camping permit, continue along the north road for 4 miles (6.4 km) and turn right onto the McManus Access Road. Drive a good 5 miles (8 km) down the bumpy dirt road, leave your pick-up vehicle at the designated parking lot, and then head back to Achray Road. Now, head to the access point by turning right and driving 29 miles (47 km) to the Algonquin Radio Observatory area. Soon after passing the observatory gate, turn right onto the side road that leads to Lake Travers.

The put-in is downstream from an iron bridge, directly below Poplar Rapids. Dave, Peter, Scott and I took advantage of the bellowing water at the base of the rapids to practice our paddle strokes, and, geared up from playing in the froth, the hour-and-a-half trip across the expanse of Lake Travers seemed monotonous. The anticipation of the downstream run forced us to race across to where Travers narrows and the flat water is pinched through a steep-sided, V-shaped valley. Eventually we could hear the vague rumble of water echoing off the rocks, marking the first run — Thompson Rapids.

The water level was low from lack of rain, exposing a few too many jagged boulders at the outset of the Thompson Dam; so Scott and I lifted the canoe around the first drop (a 380-yard [345 m] portage on the right avoids the

Lower Petawawa River

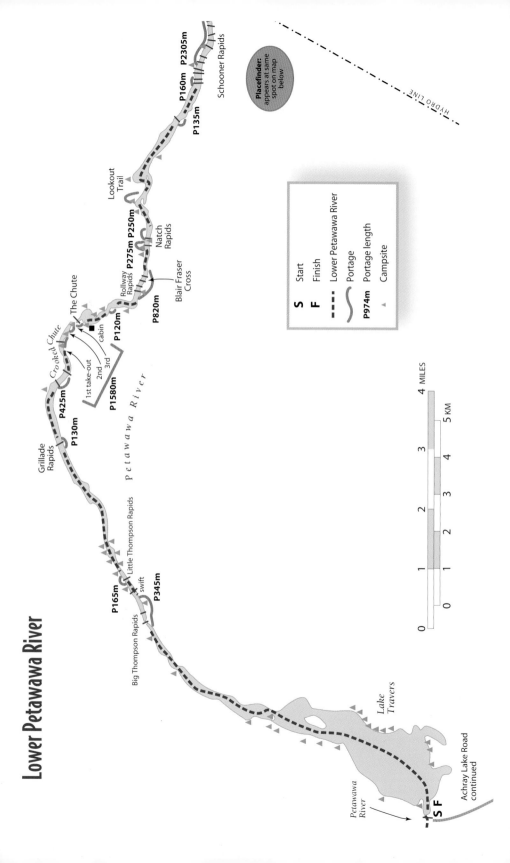

Placefinder: appears at same spot on map below

HYDRO LINE

Schooner Rapids

P160m P2305m

P135m

Lookout Trail

P275m P250m

Natch Rapids

Rollway Rapids

Blair Fraser Cross

P820m

The Chute

P120m

cabin

Crooked Chute

1st take-out
2nd
3rd

P1580m

P425m

P130m

Grillade Rapids

P e t a w a w a   R i v e r

Little Thompson Rapids

swift

P165m

P345m

Big Thompson Rapids

Lake Travers

Petawawa River

S F

Achray Lake Road continued

S Start
F Finish
      Lower Petawawa River
      Portage
P974m Portage length
▲ Campsite

MILES
4   3   2   1   0

KM
5   4   3   2   1   0

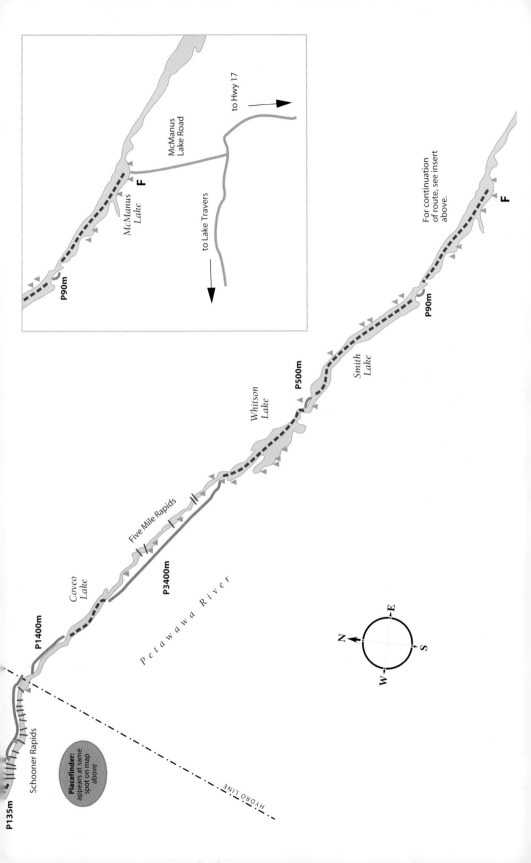

to Hwy 17

McManus
Lake Road

to Lake Travers

F

McManus
Lake

P90m

For continuation
of route, see insert
above.

F

P90m

Smith
Lake

P500m

Whitson
Lake

Five Mile Rapids

P3400m

Coveo
Lake

P1400m

P e t a w a w a   R i v e r

N

E

S

W

Schooner Rapids

P135m

Placefinder:
appears at same
spot on map
above

HYDRO LINE

entire rapid), plucked it down directly below the chute, and then walked ahead with the gear to scout what remained. On our way back upstream, firm in our conviction to take the canoe through, we noticed that another pair of trippers had parked their canoe beside ours. Dressed to the hilt — with purple PFDs, blaze-orange drysuits and metallic helmets — they stood high up on a rock, blurting out their planned route through the white stuff.

Scott and I were a little uneasy about having an audience for our first run of the trip. But when we courteously invited the other group to go first they wouldn't hear of it; so we took the plunge.

Our first maneuver was a back ferry across to the opposite bank. Then, we eddied in behind a boulder, twisted around, shot down a narrow channel, and side-slipped to the right, missing the bottom ledge by half a paddle length. All along, our high-pitched voices communicating each urgent move. If Scott pried with his paddle at the bow, I pulled mine toward me to shift the canoe sideways. As payment for our teamwork, the rapid spit us out at the end, still upright.

The other canoeists were not as successful. They bounced down the center of the run like a pinball, and by the time they reached the final drop, their canoe drifting sideways with the current and their hands gripping the gunwales, the river took control and tossed them into the drink.

About a five-minute paddle farther downriver, our group exited the canoes to survey Little Thompson Rapids, carrying our packs over the steep but short 180-yard (165 m) portage to the left. Low water still exposed the odd boulder, but this time we attached the lining ropes to the bow and stern and walked the canoe down the left bank.

Below the Thompson Rapid, the current slows for approximately 4 miles (6 km), and is interrupted only by a small swift and Grillade Rapids (graded as level I whitewater). These can easily be run, but they are also equipped with portages (140 and 465 yards [130 and 425 m], both marked to the right). Next, however, is Crooked Chute — a dangerous piece of river no matter what the water level. At its base is a collection of battered canoes that attests to the river's ferocity.

If you are unsure of your skill level, take out at the marked 1,730-yard (1,580 m) portage on the right bank. Skilled canoeists, however, can paddle the upper stretch and take advantage of a second take-out 440 yards (400 m) downstream, or even a third take-out at a campsite just before the chute itself. The remaining 660 yards (600 m) of trail splits soon after the campsite. The main trail is to the right and leads away from the river up a steep knoll.

We had planned to stay at the old rangers' cabin — built in the early 1920s and probably the oldest cabin left standing in the park — at the base of Crooked Chute. But somehow the fanatics in the metallic helmets beat us to it. With all the other campsites at Crooked Chute occupied as well, we continued downstream, running a short swift (a 130-yard [120 m] portage is marked to the right), and then pitching our tents at a poorer campsite at the take-out for Rollway Rapids.

Rollway is one of the most technical rapids on the river, and with the water levels being low, making the run a shallow, sloppy mess littered with unseen rocks, Dave and I decided to carry the canoes across the 900-yard (820 m) portage before dinner.

After slowly lowering our heavy canoes down the slippery rocks at the put-in, there was still enough evening light to head out in search of the side-trail leading to the Blair Frazer memorial. The metal cross anchored in cement commemorates the journalist and past member of a group of canoeists the Ottawa press dubbed "the Voyageurs." Frazer drowned during a spring trip in 1968, when he missed the landing and capsized in the cold water. Take note that a vandal — labeled the "Memorial Monkey Wrencher" — removed the cross in 2008, believing such memorials had no place in a wilderness setting. It's an interesting debate. I think it was an arrogant and ignorant act. In a letter to me, with no return address and written in some secret code, the culprit admitted to me vandalism and noted he had placed his own memento somewhere else in the park — he did the same thing but by his own rules. That's a blind selfish act if you ask me.

Soon after Rollway is a double set of rapids called "the Natch." Both sections have portages (300 and 275 yards [275 and 250 m]) marked on the left bank, the first being the more rugged.

The campsite close to the take-out of the first portage was a favorite haunt of the late Bill Mason. The canoeist, filmmaker and artist spent time at the Natch gathering footage for his films for the National Film Board. It was here, under the overhanging cedars opposite the impressive cliff, that the cover photograph for Mason's *Song of the Paddle* was taken, by his son, Paul.

In *Path of the Paddle*, Mason's first book of the series, he gives a horrific account of an accidental drowning on the Petawawa:

> As I was scooping a pail of water from the river I looked up and saw a bright orange object at the base of the rapids. I groaned aloud and said to Ken, [Ken Buck was Mason's cameraman] "There's a packsack out there that some poor guy's lost. I better go out and get it before it sinks." As I

neared the object, my heart nearly stopped. The orange packsack took on the shape of a life jacket and the purple shape within it became a man's face. For a split second, all the energy drained out of me.

Mason and another canoeist pulled the man from the river, and, with the help of the victim's partner, who had by then made his way to the scene, the group spent hours trying to revive him, to no avail.

Mason uses the ghastly story to emphasize the importance of proper landing procedures at a portage before a set of rapids. Apparently, the drowning occurred after the canoeists, wishing to avoid running the rapids altogether, pulled up at the portage bow-first. Immediately, the stern swung out into the current, causing the stern paddler to lose his balance and dumping him into the cold water. He was quickly swept into the main stream and was sucked under by the avalanche of whitewater waiting below.

Downstream from the Natch is pure bliss! After a 2.5-mile (4 km) section of flat water, interrupted only by two swifts (the first with a 150-yard [135 m] portage to the right, and the second with a 175-yard [160 m] portage to the left), are Schooner and Five Mile Rapids. Schooner Rapids has two portages (2,520 and 1,530 yards [2,305 and 1,400 m]) on the left bank, separated by a calm section just past a bridge and under a hydro line. Five Mile Rapids has a portage (3,720 yards [3,400 m]) on the right, with the put-in on the southwest end of Coveo Lake. The beauty of this 5-mile (8 km) stretch of whitewater, interspersed between sections of swifts, is that the rapids are only rated as level I and II, making them runnable during both high- and low-water conditions. The lengthy portage trails are in place for canoeists who, for some reason, are making their way upriver, or for inexperienced paddlers who have miraculously made it this far to escape the remaining stretch unscathed.

Being a little timid of the Petawawa ourselves, we found it hard to believe that people would even think about attempting the river without having even attempted a single flatwater trip. But it happens; in fact, far too often.

Our most memorable encounter with neophyte paddlers was during our second evening on the river. We chose the first site marked along the Five Mile portage. Just before dusk, four bedraggled canoeists strolled into camp. Apparently, they had misjudged the sizable haystack waves during the first 330 yards (300 m) of the rapid. All four of them were thrown from their boat — a 17-foot Grumman — just before a pile of jagged rocks punched several holes through the aluminum.

By the time they reached us, they had left their canoe for dead and were staggering toward the road, a good distance down-stream, drunk as skunks on a bottle of dark rum. Dave, a wizard with duct tape, helped repair the smashed canoe, and we offered them room to pitch their tents. Come morning our neighbors were still in high spirits, and we left the misfits to fend for themselves.

Our last day was spent, more often than not, wading in the cold river. Overnight, the water level had dropped substantially, and our route down the remaining rapids often involved hauling the boats along grassy cut banks and over gravel riffles.

Eventually, though, the river spilled out into Whitson Lake, where the Petawawa's northern rugged charm is softened by stands of silver maple and basswood — tree species common to more southern climes. We paddled south through Smith and McManus Lakes, easily running the two swifts en route (the first with a 550-yard [500 m] portage marked to the left and the second with a 100-yard [90 m] portage marked to the right).

By mid-afternoon, we reached the take-out at the southwestern end of McManus Lake, and when we returned from Lake Travers with the second vehicle, we were able to witness the fabulous four heading across McManus Lake in their leaky boat. By now, the rum, and their vigor, had worn off, and they paddled with an air of humility.

Lower Petawawa River

TIME
3 to 4 days

DIFFICULTY
Even though most rapids can be run, whitewater experience is mandatory (check water levels before heading out).

PORTAGES
15

LONGEST PORTAGE
3,700 yards (3,400 m)
Take note that rapids can easily be run.

Taking it easy on Algonquin's Oxtongue River.

Oxtongue River

LOOKING THROUGH THE HISTORY BOOKS, YOU MIGHT COME to believe that everyone who has ever visited Algonquin, before and even after the provincial park was formed, first paddled into the region by way of the Oxtongue River. Lieutenant Henry Briscoe became the first-recorded white person to travel the Oxtongue in 1826 while searching for a secure military route between Lake Huron and the Ottawa River. (The project was abandoned due to the river's numerous falls and rapids). Alexander Sherriff attempted to promote settlement in the region during a trip in 1829; David Thompson mapped the waterway in 1837. He was followed in 1853 by Alexander Murray, the first chief ranger of Algonquin, who traveled up to Canoe Lake in 1893 to construct the first park headquarters. Well-known artist Tom Thomson camped along the Oxtongue when he first visited the park in 1912.

More recently, however, you'd be hard-pressed to spot many other canoeists traveling the river. I'm not sure why. It could be because of its close proximity to busy Highway 60 (traffic can be heard along some sections) or maybe because canoeists believe the park has more to offer elsewhere. Whatever the reason, however, I find it one of the most rewarding weekend jaunts Algonquin has to offer — so much so, I even wonder why the heck I'm telling you about it.

There are various places to begin your trip down the Oxtongue, but the Canoe Lake access point seems to be the overall favorite. First, however, a second vehicle must be dropped off at the preferred take-out point — Algonquin Outfitters (705-635-2243) — which is located on Oxtongue Lake, just west of the Highway 60 bridge. After making arrangements to leave your car at the outfitters' parking lot, head back out to the highway and drive east toward the park (Algonquin Outfitters may provide a shuttle). The road leading off Highway 60 to the Canoe Lake access point is marked to the left, 9.5 miles (14 km) past the West Gate. You can either put in at the beach site or at the docks beside the Portage Store.

Not far out on Canoe Lake, the route heads southwest across Bonita Lake and Tea Lake. Don't be fooled by the crowds here. Daytrippers from Canoe Lake and campers from Camp Tamakwa (founded in 1937 by Lou H. Handler of Detroit) and the Tea Lake Campground (an alternative access point) can make canoe traffic a bit hectic at times. Once you get to the far end of Tea Lake and take the 262-yard (240 m) portage marked to the right of Tea Lake Dam, however, the crowds quickly disappear.

Tea Lake Dam was where artist Tom Thomson made camp while on his first visit to Algonquin. The trip was to be a warmup to his two-month expedition down the Mississagi River. He later returned to Tea Lake Dam in 1914 to paint, and even guided fellow artist A. Y. Jackson to the very same spot.

You'll encounter only a couple of small swifts on the river before reaching another historic stop — Whiskey Rapids. Here, sometime near the turn of the century, two log-drivers lost a three-gallon keg of whiskey. They were appointed by their fellow workers to head up the Oxtongue to pick up the precious cargo at the Canoe Lake Railway Station. Everything was going as planned, that is, until they decided to stop for a drink or two on their return trip. It was dark by the time they reached the rapid, and, having spotted the take-out for the portage at the last minute, the drunkards chose to run down the whitewater while it was in spring flood. They made it but the barrel of whiskey was never found.

The present-day portage around Whiskey Rapids is an easy 209 yards (190 m) and is marked to the right. Just be sure to keep to the left when the trail forks halfway along.

Downstream, not far past another shallow rapid that can be either run or waded down, depending on water levels, the waterway begins to meander all over. This calm stretch of river, winding its way around pine-clad bluffs on one side and spilling quietly past islands covered in alder and dogwood on the other, is a great place to spot a moose, especially in early spring when almost every salt-deprived moose in the park is attracted to the road salt left along the highway close by.

It will take about an hour's paddle from Whiskey Rapids before the footbridge for the Western Uplands Hiking Trail comes into view. This is another possible access point for canoeists looking for a much shorter weekend on the Oxtongue. And from there, it's another hour's paddle before the river picks up speed again, first at a series of insignificant swifts and then, shortly after, at the more noteworthy Upper and Lower Twin Falls and Split Rock Rapids. Both cascades have short portages (262 yards and 110 yards [240 m, 100 m], each marked to the left). However, the take-out for Split Rock Rapids is incredibly steep and is uncomfortably close to the edge of the falls, especially during high-water levels. So you may want to play it safe and head for shore a few yards further upstream to make use of an extended bush trail.

The river continues to meander for another three hours, passing by what Alexander Sherriff perfectly described in his 1829 journal as "A level, sandy valley, timbered chiefly with balsam, tamarac, and poplar, beyond which,

Moose calf, Oxtongue River

however, the hardwood rising grounds are seen seldom a mile distant on either side." Then, not far past where Algonquin Provincial Park ends and Oxtongue River/Ragged Falls Provincial Park begins (the border is marked by a small creek on the left that leads to the nearby highway), the river drops down five sets of shallow rapids before plunging over the 33-foot-high (10 m) Gravel Falls.

All five rapids can be run. The first and fourth each have a portage

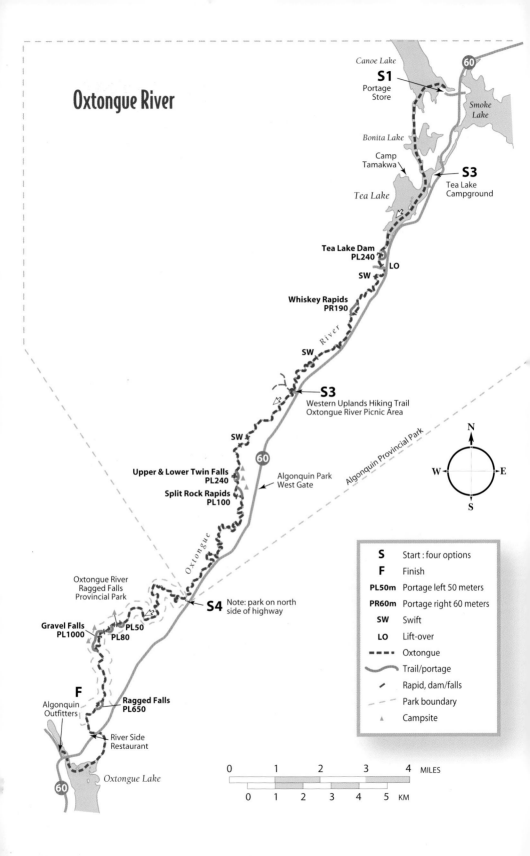

Oxtongue River

Canoe Lake

S1
Portage Store

Smoke Lake

60

Bonita Lake

Camp Tamakwa

S3
Tea Lake Campground

Tea Lake

Tea Lake Dam PL240
LO
SW

Whiskey Rapids PR190

SW

River

S3
Western Uplands Hiking Trail
Oxtongue River Picnic Area

SW

60

Upper & Lower Twin Falls PL240

Algonquin Park West Gate

Split Rock Rapids PL100

Oxtongue

Oxtongue River Ragged Falls Provincial Park

S4 Note: park on north side of highway

Gravel Falls PL1000
PL50
PL80

F

Algonquin Outfitters

Ragged Falls PL650

River Side Restaurant

Oxtongue Lake

60

Algonquin Provincial Park

N
W — E
S

S	Start : four options
F	Finish
PL50m	Portage left 50 meters
PR60m	Portage right 60 meters
SW	Swift
LO	Lift-over
----	Oxtongue
~~	Trail/portage
⌐	Rapid, dam/falls
---	Park boundary
▲	Campsite

0   1   2   3   4 MILES

0   1   2   3   4   5 KM

(55 yards and 88 yards [50 m, 80 m]) marked on the left just in case. You may also want to wade down the fifth set, which is only a few yards above the brink of the falls.

Gravel Falls comes with a long, 1,100-yard (1,000 m) portage, marked to the right. Don't worry — experienced whitewater paddlers can put in directly below the falls (reducing the portage to 220 yards [200 m]), and even we mere mortals have to carry only about halfway and then can run the swift water that remains.

The current continues its fast pace all the way to Ragged Falls, located about another half hour downriver. This is an even more scenic cascade than Gravel Falls — dropping three times its height — but it's also a day-use area, and I find the trip quickly loses its wilderness appeal the moment you run into the crowds of tourists who walk in from the highway. As well, the network of trails leading back and forth from the falls make finding the exact whereabouts of the portage (710 yards [650 m] and marked to the left) extremely frustrating. There are, however, small florescent squares on the trees to help point you in the right direction.

From Ragged Falls it's an easy paddle to the Highway 60 bridge, where you can pull into the unique River Side Restaurant for coffee and cake. From here, you simply continue for another twenty minutes, out into the expanse of Oxtongue Lake. By keeping to the right-hand shore, you'll eventually paddle under the Highway 60 bridge again, and then take out at the familiar Algonquin Outfitters to your left.

Oxtongue River

TIME
2 days

DIFFICULTY
Moderate to novice

PORTAGES
11

LONGEST PORTAGE
1,100 yards (1,000 m) (can be easily reduced to 220 yards [200 m] by running some rapids below Gravel Falls)

The Windigo to Radiant Lake canoe route is one of the most accessible canoe routes Algonquin's east end has to offer.

Windigo to Radiant Lake

I'VE PADDLED FROM THE WINDIGO ACCESS POINT THROUGH to Radiant Lake a couple of times on the way to begin a trip down the notable Petawawa River but my mind had always been on the whitewater awaiting me on the river section that starts after Radiant, not on the series of lakes leading up to it. So I decided to return to the area and paddle from Windigo to Radiant and back to see what I had missed along the way. By doing so I discovered one of the best quick and easy trips Algonquin's east end has to offer.

My canoe mate, Andy Baxter, and I chose the first weekend in October for the trip. Trout season had just closed but some of the lakes en route were populated with bass and walleye, and October is prime time for catching either species.

The access point is reached by turning south off Highway 17, just west of Deux Rivières, on the Brent Road. The permit office is just down the gravel road. From there it's a 10 mile (16 km) drive down Brent Road and then left onto the Windigo Lake access road. It's another couple of miles to the launch site.

Since I live in Peterborough, Ontario it was a long drive for us to reach the east end of the park, making it mid-morning by the time we paddled off from the canoe launch. Windigo Lake isn't part of the park yet. The Algonquin border doesn't start until the first portage (taking us to Allan Lake) on the far eastern end of Windigo. The portage measured 195 yards (180 m) and was an easy carry. So was the second, a 280-yard (255 m) carry into North Depot Lake. In fact, we found most of the portages on this route relatively straight-forward. Problem was, the campsites on Allan Lake and North Depot Lake showed some abuse because of it. The sites themselves were nice but the majority of them, especially the ones on the main islands, were devoid of good firewood. The scenery here is still spectacular, with the typical stout white pine rooted along a granite shoreline and loons serenading while we paddled. It's one of the many gems Algonquin has to offer.

It was lunch break by the time we reached the end of North Depot Lake and Andy and I snacked on cheese and dried salami before taking on the longest portage en route — 840 yards (770 m) running along the left side of a set of rapids and ending at an old dam. The put-in marks my favorite part of the route — the North River. You're almost guaranteed to see a moose here. This time we saw two; a bull and later a cow. I've seen a lot of moose

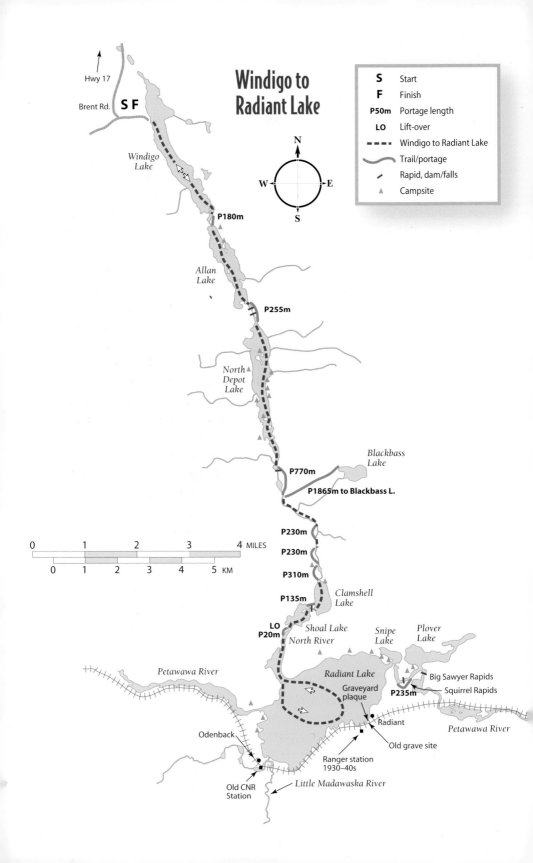

Windigo to Radiant Lake

Hwy 17

Brent Rd. **S F**

Windigo Lake

P180m

Allan Lake

P255m

North Depot Lake

Blackbass Lake

P770m

P1865m to Blackbass L.

P230m

P230m

P310m

P135m

Clamshell Lake

LO
P20m

Shoal Lake

North River

Snipe Lake

Plover Lake

Petawawa River

Radiant Lake

Big Sawyer Rapids

Squirrel Rapids

P235m

Graveyard plaque

Radiant

Old grave site

Petawawa River

Odenback

Ranger station
1930–40s

Old CNR
Station

Little Madawaska River

0	1	2	3	4	MILES
0	1	2	3	4	5 KM

Legend

S Start
F Finish
P50m Portage length
LO Lift-over
- - - Windigo to Radiant Lake
～ Trail/portage
／ Rapid, dam/falls
▲ Campsite

N
W — E
S

in my previous canoe journeys but these two meant something a little more special to me. Prior to the trip my daughter, now seven, had reminded me that she had yet to see a moose even though she's been paddling the north with me since she was six weeks old! I'm not sure why we've never spotted a moose on our trips but she's always disappointed we haven't. So, before my trip, I promised her I would find one and take a few photos for her. I also read her a quote from Bill Bryson's A Walk in the Woods — "Hunters will tell you that a moose is a wily and ferocious forest creature. Nonsense. A moose is a cow drawn by a three-year old." She giggled uncontrollably after hearing that and insisted that I find one for her and take a picture. That day she got her wish and I became the best dad ever — for a whole week at least.

Three portages followed (250 yard, 250 yard and 340 yard [230 m, 230 m and 310 m]) , pretty much one after the other along the right side of the North River before reaching a small pond named Clamshell Lake. Just make sure to stay on the trail of the second portage to the very end and don't get misled by a faint trail that leads you back to the river too early.

There was only one campsite on Clamshell, on the east end on top a big mound of rock, and even though it was small, with room for one tent, it seemed perfect. We had planned to get all the way to Radiant, however, so we paddled quickly across to the other side, stopping briefly to cast a line for smallmouth bass under the fallen timber lining the banks and caught four good size fish. Then we took on two more short portages — 147 yards (135 m) to Shoal Lake and a very quick 22 yards (20 m) around a beaver dam — back to North River where it flows into Radiant Lake.

Radiant Lake was worth the effort. But it took awhile before we realized it. It's a big, round, shallow lake, which makes for rough water when the wind is blowing. And the wind was blowing when we arrived. Exploring the lake became next to impossible. We simply hugged the shoreline looking for a campsite and on the north end discovered an incredible beach and called it a day. Later in the evening the wind calmed down and we ended up spending a glorious evening sipping bush martinis on the beach and watching the sun set along the west shore.

The next morning we awoke to a motor boat buzzing across Radiant. Andy and I had forgotten that motors of 10 horsepower or less are allowed on the lake. There are also a few rustic cottages on Radiant's northwestern shoreline. The owners arrive by an old road or the abandoned CNR railway line. Personally, this intrusion didn't take away from our wild surroundings at all. In fact, Radiant Lake is far less busy now than in the past. When the railway was here this was a main access point for canoeists entering the

*A late season trip in Algonquin
has the advantage of having far less crowds.*

park. The authors of the well noted Algonquin book *The Incomplete Anglers* (1944) began their trek across the park by jumping off the train here. The train station was west of where the Petawawa River flushes into the lake. The park's office, run by legendary park ranger Zeph Nadon, was located on the opposite corner of the lake. Nadon was one of the park rangers asked to apprehend Grey Owl (Archie Belaney) who, on a bet, decided to protest the rules of no trapping in the park and headed across Algonquin in midwinter. He was caught, actually saved, by the rangers after falling through the ice. Zeph's son later went on to become one of Canada's top RCMP officers. The original land surveyor of the Algonquin region, J. MacDonell, also noted that Radiant Lake (then named Trout Lake) had numerous camps of the Algonquins when he stopped to purchase a canoe from them in 1847. It was during the logging era, however, that Radiant Lake saw the largest amount of traffic. Various lumber companies, including J.R. Booth, Gillies Bros. and Bronson Co., worked around the lake — especially in the 1930s. A large depot farm was constructed along the west shore and a steam powered tug boomed logs into the bay of the North River.

Andy and I spent the entire next day exploring Radiant Lake. In the morning we fished for smallmouth bass and walleye, especially at the mouth of the Petawawa River. We even took a 256-yard (235 m) portage down stream on the Petawawa to Plover Lake where we caught some amazing bass.

Later in the day we circumnavigated the lake and checked out the logger's gravesite noted on our park map. The graves themselves weren't easy to find but we found the memorial plaque easily enough. Located on the southeast corner of the lake, placed on a large boulder up from a beach, states "In this enclosure are buried the bodies of more than twenty rivermen drowned in the nearby waters before 1916 when the railway was completed." From the plaque we followed a faint trail to the east, through an alder thicket, which ends up at the Bissett/Radiant Road. According to information gathered from Donald Lloyd's book *Canoeing Algonquin Park* (2000), an even fainter trail to the left will lead to a wooden staff that marks the whereabouts of a single wooden cross held together with binder twine. Andy and I found the side trail but no evidence of a wooden staff or graves. I'm guessing too much time has passed and anything that remained has blended in with the forest.

Our third night was to be our last and Andy and I paddled the same route backwards to stay on an island site on North Depot Lake. This allowed us to be closer to the access point and get an early start on the long drive home. It also provided a nice change. North Depot Lake is much smaller than Radiant and it was satisfying to be away from the harsh winds. In retrospect, however, Andy and I missed Radiant Lake and around the campfire our last night out, while once again sipping bush martinis and watching the sun set, we planned a return trip to Radiant. It's a captivating place — and besides, next time we just might find the hidden gravesites that escaped us the first time out.

Windigo to Radiant Lake

TIME
3–4 days

DIFFICULTY
Novice to moderate

PORTAGES
16

LONGEST PORTAGE
840 yards

Algonquin Guides/Outfitters

CEDAR LAKE
Algonquin Outfitters —
Brent Store
R.R. 1, Hwy. 60
Dwight, Ontario
P0A 1H0
705-635-2243 or 1-800-469-4948
www.algonquinoutfitters.com

EAST END
Algonquin Portage
R.R. 6
Pembroke, Ontario
K8A 6W7
613-735-1795
www.algonquinportage.com

Trips and Trails
Adventure Outfitting
Box 1650
258 Hastings St. N
Bancroft, Ontario
K0L 1C0
613-332-1969
http://tripsandtrails.ca

Algonquin Bound
525 Barron Canyon Road
Pembroke, Ontario
www.algonquinbound.com
1-800-704-4537

HIGHWAY 60 CORRIDOR
Algonquin Outfitters
R.R. 1, Hwy 60
Dwight, Ontario
P0A 1H0
1-800-469-4948
www.algonquinoutfitters.com

The Portage Store
c/o Huntsville P.O.
Huntsville, Ontario
P0A 1K0
705-633-5622 or 705-789 3645
www.portagestore.com

Algonquin Outfitters —
Opeongo Store
R.R. 1
Dwight, Ontario
P0A 1H0
613-637-2075 or 1-888-280-8886
www.algonquinoutfitters.com
* provides water taxi service
for Lake Opeongo

Opeongo Outfitters
Box 123
Whitney, Ontario
K0J 2M0
613-637-5470 or 1-800-790-1864
www.opeongooutfitters.com
* provides water taxi service for
Lake Opeongo

Algonquin Bound
Highway 60 & Major Lake Road
Madawaska, Ontario
www.algonquinbound.com
1-800-704-4537

KAWAWAYMOG LAKE (ROUND LAKE)
Voyageur Outfitting
Box 67055
Toronto, Ontario
M4P 1E0
416-488-6175
or
Box 69
South River, Ontario
P0A 1X0
705-386-2813 (July/August)
or 1-877-837-8889
www.voyageuroutfitting.com

Northern Wilderness Outfitters
Box 89
South River, Ontario
P0A 1X0
705-386-0466 (summer)
or 705-474-3272
or 1-888-368-6123
www.northernwilderness.com

Swift Outdoor Centre
Swift South River
(Visitor's Information Centre)
281 Highway 11 North
South River
705-386-0440
http://swiftoutdoorcentres.com/
stores/southriver.php

Voyageur Quest
22 Belcourt Road
Toronto, Ontario
M4S 2T9
416-486-3605 or 1-800-794-9660
www.voyageurquest.com

Northern Edge Algonquin
1-800-953-3343
northernedgealgonquin@gmail.com
www.northernedgealgonquin.com

KIOSK LAKE
Algonquin North
Wilderness Outfitters
corner of Hwy 17 and Hwy 630
Mattawa, Ontario
P0H 1V0
705-744-3265 or 1-877-544-3544
www.algonquinnorth.com

WEST END
Canoe Algonquin
1914 Hwy 518 East
Kearney, Ontario,
Canada
705-636-5956 or 1-800-818-1210
www.canoealgonquin.com

Algonquin Outfitters —
Huntsville Store
86 Main St. E.
Huntsville, ON
P1H 1C7
705-787-0262 or 1-800-469-4948
www.algonquinoutfitters.com

Algonquin Bound
5280 Hwy. 60
Dwight, Ontario
www.algonquinbound.com
1-800-704-4537

SHALL LAKE AREA
Algonquin Bound
Madawaska, Ontario
613-637-5508 or 1-800-704-4537
info@algonquinbound.com
www.algonquinbound.com

RESERVATION SYSTEM
www.ontarioparks.com
www.ontarioparks.com
Reservations for Algonquin Park:
1-888-668-7275

ALGONQUIN PARK INFORMATION / FRIENDS OF ALGONQUIN PARK
www.algonquinpark.on.ca
Algonquin Park information,
campsite availability and route
information: 705-633-5572

Bibliography

Addison, Ottelyn. *Early Days in Algonquin Park.* Toronto; New York: McGraw-Hill Ryerson, 1974.

Bice, Ralph. *Along the Trail with Ralph Bice in Algonquin Park.* Scarborough, Ont.: Consolidated Amethyst, 1980.

Brown, Ron. *50 Unusual Things to See in Ontario.* Erin: The Boston Mills Press, 1981.

Cundiff, Brad. "Not Out of the Woods . . . Yet." *Seasons,* spring 1993.

Dawson, Blair. "Algonquin's Very Special Specks." *Ontario Out of Doors,* July 1995.

Dewdney, Selwyn and Kenneth E. Kidd. *Indian Rock Paintings of the Great Lakes.* Toronto: University of Toronto Press, 1973.

Drought, George. *Petawawa River Whitewater Guide: Algonquin Provincial Park.* Whitney: The Friends of Algonquin Provincial Park, 1993.

Egan, Kelly. "Why Don't Bears Kill More People?" *The Spectator,* summer 1996.

Friends Of Algonquin Park. *Canoe Routes of Algonquin Park* [map]. 1996.

Gage, S.R. *A Few Rustic Huts: Ranger Cabins and Logging Camp Buildings of Algonquin Park.* Oakville: Mosaic Press, 1985.

Garland, G.D. *Glimpses of Algonquin: Thirty Personal Impressions from Earliest Times to the Present.* Whitney: Friends of Algonquin Park, 1994.

Kates, Joanne. *Exploring Algonquin Park.* Vancouver: Douglas & McIntyre, 1983.

Lundell, Liz. *Algonquin: The Park And Its People.* Toronto: McClelland & Stewart, 1993.

——— *Summer Camps: Great Camps of Algonquin Park.* Erin: The Boston Mills Press, 1994.

Mason, Bill. *Path of the Paddle: An Illustrated Guide to the Art of Canoeing.* Toronto: Key Porter Press, 1984.

——— *Song of the Paddle: An Illustrated Guide to Wilderness Camping.* Toronto: Key Porter Press, 1988.

Ministry of Natural Resources. *Algonquin Logging Museum: Logging in Algonquin Park.* 1993.

——— *Names of Algonquin: Algonquin Park Technical Bulletin No. 10.* 1991.

Rand, Mac, *Paddles Flashing in the Sun: The Stories of Pathfinder in Algonquin Park.* New York, 1995.

Runtz, Michael. *The Explorer's Guide to Algonquin Park.* Erin: The Boston Mills Press, 1993, 2008.

Saunders, Audrey. *Algonquin Story.* Toronto: Ontario Department of Lands and Forest, 1963.

Strickland, Dan and Russ Rutter. *The Best of the Raven.* Whitney: Friends of Algonquin Park, 1993.

Tesher, Ellie. "Experts Offer to Re-examine Artist's Death." *The Toronto Star,* August 19, 1996.

Tozer, Ron. *A Pictorial History of Algonquin Provincial Park.* Whitney: Published in cooperation with the Ontario Ministry of Natural Resources by the Friends of Algonquin Park, 1991.